# Addressing the Challenges for Asset-backed Pensions in Indonesia

OECD

BETTER POLICIES FOR BETTER LIVES

**Please cite this publication as:**
OECD (2025), *Addressing the Challenges for Asset-backed Pensions in Indonesia*, OECD Publishing, Paris, https://doi.org/10.1787/37f4700d-en.

ISBN 978-92-64-91231-1 (print)
ISBN 978-92-64-53844-3 (PDF)
ISBN 978-92-64-91018-8 (HTML)

**Photo credits:** Cover © ferlistockphoto/Getty Images.

Corrigenda to OECD publications may be found at: https://www.oecd.org/en/publications/support/corrigenda.html.

# Foreword

The design and regulation of asset-backed pension systems provide a framework for individuals to build sufficient resources to finance their retirement. Nevertheless, protection gaps resulting in insufficient retirement savings may still arise. One driver of these protection gaps is that the rules of the system may sometimes be inadequate to allow the population to achieve the desired objectives for retirement, appropriate schemes or vehicles may be unavailable and individuals may not necessarily make use of those that are. Additional challenges may impede the system from delivering the targeted retirement outcomes. This can lead to retirement savings gaps that can leave individuals under-protected and put their financial well-being in retirement at risk.

This report draws from the work of the OECD Working Party on Insurance and Pensions on asset-backed pensions, contributing to the dissemination of OECD standards and recommendations relating to pensions and learning from international practices. It also contributes to the Working Party's regional outreach in Asia in the context of the annual OECD-ADBI Roundtable on Insurance and Retirement Savings in Asia. The report provides lessons from the experience of the asset-backed pension system in Indonesia, along with insights into the challenges that it faces and the policy options available to address these challenges based on international good practices.

This report has been developed by the Capital Markets and Financial Institutions Division of the OECD Directorate for Financial and Enterprise Affairs. It was prepared by Jessica Mosher under the supervision of Pablo Antolín, Head of the Insurance and Pensions Unit, and Serdar Çelik, Head of Division.

The OECD gratefully acknowledges financial support from the Government of Japan that made the preparation of this report possible. The report has also benefited from valuable exchanges and collaboration with the Indonesian Financial Services Authority.

On 20 February 2024, the OECD Council decided to open accession discussions with Indonesia. The Roadmap for the OECD Accession Process of Indonesia was adopted on 29 March 2024. In accordance with the Roadmap, Indonesia will undergo in-depth reviews by the OECD technical committees listed in the Roadmap. This report is separate from Indonesia's accession process and does not prejudge the recommendations that may be suggested in the process.

# Table of contents



## FIGURES

## TABLES

# Executive summary

The Indonesian pension system faces numerous challenges to providing adequate retirement benefits for its population. While the introduction of the mandatory asset-backed pension schemes for private-sector workers in 2015 was a significant step towards improving access to pension schemes for the Indonesian population, many categories of workers remain underserved and have fewer opportunities to save for their retirement. The rules relating to benefit accruals and the withdrawals of retirement savings occasionally fail to incentivise saving or provide adequate benefits in retirement. Additionally, occupational pension plans are being closed, and vehicles to protect retirees from longevity risk are not widely available. Furthermore, even when saving for retirement is mandatory, compliance is low.

In addition to addressing the challenges leading to retirement savings protection gaps, the Indonesian pension system needs to ensure the design of the system itself is conducive to achieving its objectives. Key challenges relate to investment, sustainability, and complementarity. First, pension fund investments remain overly conservative and strategies are not appropriate to achieve optimal outcomes for members at retirement. Second, the parameters relating to the financing of defined benefit plans are inadequate to ensure their long-term solvency and sustainability. Finally, the different components of the system sometimes lack clear and complementary objectives.

To address these challenges, Indonesia should first ensure that the rules of the pension system allow individuals to accumulate adequate retirement savings. Rules for different types of workers should be more aligned in terms of contribution limits and the accrual of benefits to avoid hindering the ability of certain groups to accumulate retirement benefits. Accrual formulas should also ensure continued incentives to contribute to encourage compliance and participation in the pension schemes. Retirement ages for mandatory schemes should align to encourage workers to contribute for longer. The payout options available and their taxation should encourage individuals to take their retirement savings as regular income in retirement.

The regulatory framework should also promote the availability of options to accumulate retirement savings and provide an income in retirement. Additional measures could reduce the costs of opening and administering a plan to counter the trend to close voluntary occupational schemes. Allowing providers to offer non-guaranteed lifetime income options could promote the availability of payout vehicles offering longevity protection by limiting risk exposure to providers. A public annuity provider could also be considered to ensure the supply of lifetime income vehicles.

The authorities should also take steps to improve the uptake and use of retirement savings schemes by the population. Contributions to mandatory schemes could be better enforced by leveraging the position of the tax authority. Government-provided matching contributions could also encourage participation, in particular for low-income groups who may have a lower capacity to save.

The investment strategies of pension schemes should be more diversified and in line with the goal of financing retirement. Certain investment restrictions, such as minimum requirements for investment in government bonds and limits on foreign investment, should be relaxed. The expanded use of default lifecycle investment strategies could help to increase investment risk exposure at younger ages and increase overall investment returns in the long run. Investment performance should be measured with appropriate metrics and benchmarks that are in line with the long-term investment horizon of pension funds to promote accountability for investment results. Rules should eliminate the possibility to finance severance benefits with occupational pension funds, as this presents a conflict of interest with the objective that pension funds should have to finance the retirement benefits of employees. Finally, policy makers should strengthen requirements around investment expertise in the governance framework.

The regulatory framework also needs to strengthen the sustainability of defined benefit pension funds. For public mandatory schemes, contributions need to increase to better align with the expected benefit payments. Voluntary occupational plans should be subject to clear requirements for the valuation of their liabilities and funding calculations that better reflect their actual solvency position and ensure adequate funding levels.

Finally, schemes' design should align with clear objectives that aim to ensure complementarity of the different components of the system. Currently, the severance pay system lacks a clear objective, and it is not designed in a way that actually benefits those it intends to help, so should be replaced by increased employer contributions to the mandatory defined contribution scheme for private sector workers. Early withdrawals from the mandatory defined contribution scheme for private sector workers should only be allowed for exceptional individual circumstances to avoid savings being depleted before retirement. Finally, the objective of the new mandatory pension programme that increases contributions for higher-income employees needs clarification to ensure the alignment of its design with that objective.

The policy options included in this report, which draw on OECD guidelines and international good practices, could help the Indonesian pension system to address some of the challenges it faces and improve retirement outcomes for the population.

# 1 Retirement savings protection gaps and challenges to achieve adequate retirement outcomes

This chapter describes the financial protection gaps relating to retirement savings in Indonesia and the additional challenges the asset-backed pension system faces to delivering expected outcomes in retirement. It looks at the protection gaps relating to the rules of the system, the availability of appropriate savings instruments and payout vehicles, and the population's uptake of these vehicles. It then discusses additional challenges relating to the investment of pension funds, their solvency and sustainability, and the harmonisation and complementarity of the different components of the system.

Financial protection gaps related to retirement savings may arise from a number of drivers. The first is the extent to which the regulatory framework establishes the appropriate savings vehicles and allows for individuals to save adequately for their retirement given the limits in place. This relates to how the **rules** of the system can deliver desired retirement outcomes for the population. The second driver is the extent to which providers offer the savings vehicles established in the regulatory framework for the population to use. This relates to the **availability** of appropriate savings instruments and products. A final driver relates to the extent to which the population makes use of the available savings vehicles to adequately prepare for their retirement. This relates to the population's **uptake** and use of the instruments at their disposition to save for retirement. While these factors are the main drivers of pension protection gaps, several other challenges contribute to the system falling short in delivering expected outcomes.

This chapter describes the features of the Indonesian pension system as they relate to the three dimensions of protection gaps driven by rules, availability, and uptake. It then discusses key additional challenges relating to the investment of pension funds, their solvency and sustainability, and the harmonisation and complementarity of the system.

## 1.1. Protection gaps arising from the rules of the system

The capacity of the system to deliver adequate retirement savings depends on the rules of the system. The rules dictate to what extent individuals have access to savings plans and how much they can contribute, as well as at what age they can retire and how they can use their savings to finance retirement.

The Indonesian pension system comprises various components that cover different groups of the population.

- The tax-financed social assistance programme with a focus on assisting the elderly, Asistensi Rehabilitasi Sosial Lanjut Usia (ATENSI LU), in place since 2020.
- The tax-financed, means-tested social pension, Program Keluarga Harapan (PKH Lansia), paying quarterly benefits to persons aged 70 and over.
- The pension programme for armed forces and military personnel, Asabri, a mandatory pay-as-you-go defined benefit (DB) pension plan for all professional military personnel, civil employees of the Ministry of Defence and the police force. It is managed by PT Asabri and financed by the state budget.
- The mandatory pension programme for civil servants managed by Taspen, a state-owned enterprise. All employees contribute to the DB component, Taspen-JP. Contributions are invested and benefits are financed by government revenues since 2009. Since 2017, all employees are also required to contribute to the THT, a DC scheme.
- The mandatory pension programme for private sector employees established in 2015, managed by Badan Penyelenggara Jaminan Sosial (BPJS) Employment. It comprises a defined benefit (DB) component, Jaminan Pensiun (JP), which invests contributions net of benefit payments, and a defined contribution (DC) component, Jaminan Hari Tua (JHT), which invests contributions in a collective investment fund.
- Voluntary occupational pension plans introduced in 1992, which can be DB or DC. Employers providing a DB pension plan can set up their own pension fund (DPPK PPMP), either as a single-employer or as a multi-employer fund. Employers providing a DC pension plan can set up their own plan (DPPK PPIP) or join a pension fund provided by a financial institution (DPLK). DPPK pension funds can include both DB and DC pension plans.
- Personal voluntary pension plans available to all individuals regardless of their employment and provided by a financial institution (DPLK).

This report focuses on the asset-backed components of the pension system in Indonesia. Figure 1.1 presents them; they are all those in which contributions are invested, earn investment returns, and assets accumulated finance retirement.

### Figure 1.1. Illustration of the Indonesian asset-backed pension system

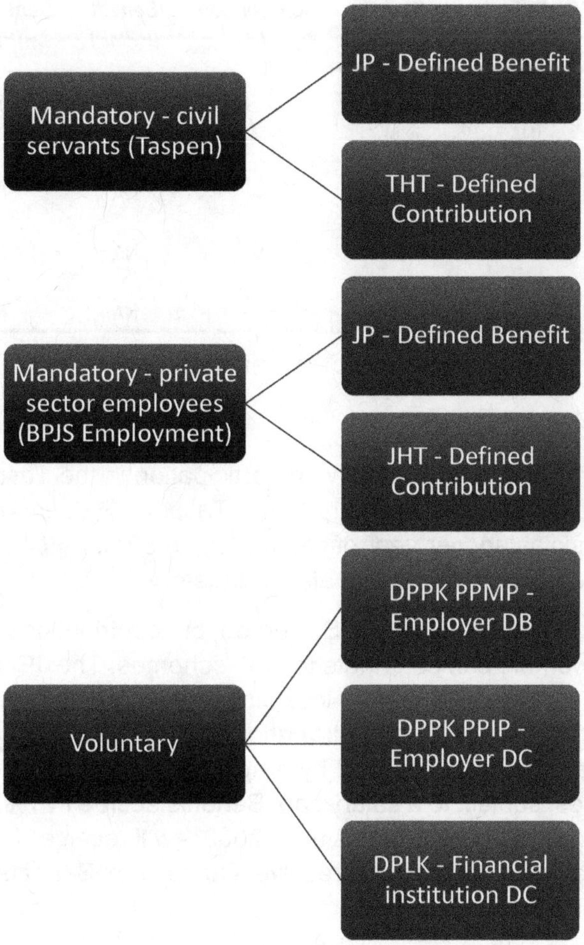


Note: The pension plan for armed forces and military personnel, Asabri, also includes a DC component. This plan is not included here.

### *1.1.1. Access and contributions to retirement savings plans*

Private-sector workers now have better access to retirement savings since the introduction of the mandatory BPJS pension schemes in 2015. Nevertheless, informal workers have fewer opportunities to save for retirement. Table 1.1 summarises the types of pension plans available to different types of workers, and indicates whether participation is mandatory or voluntary.

**Table 1.1. Pension plans available to different types of workers**

| Type of Worker | Mandatory plan for civil servants - Taspen | | Mandatory plan for private sector employees – BPJS Employment | | Voluntary employer-provided occupational plan - DPPK | | Voluntary financial institution-provided plan - DPLK | |
|---|---|---|---|---|---|---|---|---|
| | *Defined Benefit - JP* | *Defined Contribution - THT* | *Defined Benefit - JP* | *Defined Contribution - JHT* | *Defined Benefit (PPMP)* | *Defined Contribution (PPIP)* | *Occupational* | *Personal* |
| **Formal** | | | | | | | | |
| Public servant | M | M | NA | NA | NA | NA | NA | V |
| Large/medium enterprise | NA | NA | M | M | V | V | V | V |
| Small enterprise | NA | NA | NA | M | NA | NA | V | V |
| Micro enterprise | NA | NA | NA | V | NA | NA | V | V |
| **Informal** | NA | NA | NA | V | NA | NA | NA | V |

Note: M = mandatory; V = voluntary; NA = no access. Table excludes armed forces.
Source: OJK.

Civil servants are well-covered by the system, with participation in the Taspen scheme being mandatory. All civil servants contribute 4.75% of their salary to the Taspen JP defined benefit plan in which benefits accrue by 2.5% of final basic salary per year of service, up to 80%. Since 2017, contributions of 3.25% of salary to the THT defined contribution plan are also mandatory.

Private sector employees contribute to the BPJS scheme, but contributions are not mandatory for all types of employees, and not all workers can contribute to both schemes. The JP defined benefit scheme is open to employees across all business scales – including micro, small, medium, and large enterprises. Nonetheless, under prevailing regulations, participation in the JP scheme is mandatory only for medium and large enterprises. The scheme is financed by employee contributions of 1% of wages and employer contributions of 2% of wages, subject to a salary cap. Benefits accrue at 1% per year, adjusted for inflation. Those having 15 years of contributions – that is from 2030 – will receive lifetime income payments. Those not having contributed for at least 15 years will receive a lump sum. Benefits are subject to a minimum and maximum benefit and are indexed to prices.

The BPJS-JHT defined contribution plan is available to all workers and is mandatory for workers in large, medium and small enterprises. The scheme guarantees a minimum return of one year tenor of bank deposit interest. Contributions are 2% from employees and 3.7% from employers. Contributions to this scheme are voluntary for informal workers, including the self-employed who may contribute 2% of their wages. The amount that migrant workers can contribute depends on their salary levels.

Voluntary occupational pension schemes are available primarily to employees of large and medium enterprises. These plans can be DB or DC in nature. DB plans must be set up within an employer pension fund (DPPK). DC plans can be offered within an employer pension fund (DPPK) or set up through a financial institution (DPLK). Employer contributions are required for these plans, but employees do not necessarily have to contribute. In principle, any employer could set up a voluntary occupational plan, but in practice micro and small enterprises are not likely to have the resources to do so. There is no legal limitation for contributions to voluntary occupational schemes.

Access to personal pension plans is universal. All individuals regardless of employment status are allowed to contribute to a personal retirement savings plan provided by a financial institution.

The rules relating to the access to pension imply that a large proportion of the population over the age of 15 will only have access to a personal pension plan. Only working individuals in Indonesia will have access to the BPJS-JHT scheme, meaning that over 30% of the working-age population will not have access to the scheme. The total workforce in Indonesia is 143.7 million people, of which 5.9% are unemployed. The workforce represents 68.6% of the population over the age of 15 (Table 1.2). This is higher than the OECD average labour market participation rate (ages 15 and over) of 61% (ILO, 2025[1]).

### Table 1.2. Working population, August 2022

| | |
|---|---|
| Total Workforce | 143 722 644 |
| *Labour market participation* | *68.63%* |
| Unemployed | 8 425 931 |
| *Unemployment rate* | *5.86%* |
| Total Population > 15 | 209 420 383 |

Source: BPS-Statistics Indonesia (2023[2]), Labour Statistics, https://www.bps.go.id/en/statistics-table?subject=520.

Women are less likely to participate in the workforce than men, meaning that they will have lower coverage by the pension system. The rate of female participation in the labour force in 2022 was only 53.4%, compared to 83.9% for men (BPS-Statistics Indonesia, 2023[2]). This is in line with the OECD average female labour force participation rate (ages 15 and over) of 53% (ILO, 2025[1]). While all workers in Indonesia have access to a BPJS-provided pension, most are not required to participate in any retirement savings arrangement. Informal workers, who are not mandated to contribute, make up nearly 60% of the working population (Table 1.3).[1] Additionally, women are less likely to be required to contribute because they are more likely to work in informal jobs that do not require them to save for retirement than men. Sixty-four per cent of employed women were working in informal jobs in 2022, compared to 56% of employed men (BPS-Statistics Indonesia, 2023[2]).

### Table 1.3. Breakdown of formal and informal workers, 2022

| Type of worker | Number of people | % of total workforce |
|---|---|---|
| Formal, of which: | 55 052 233 | 40.7% |
| *Large/medium enterprise* | *45 635 454* | *82.9%* |
| *Small enterprise* | *1 959 837* | *3.6%* |
| *Micro enterprise* | *7 456 942* | *13.6%* |
| Informal | 80 244 480 | 59.3% |

Note: Split of public/private sector not available, and public sector workers and the armed forces and military are included in the count of large/medium enterprises.
Source: BPS-Statistics Indonesia (2023[2]), Labour Statistics, https://www.bps.go.id/en/statistics-table?subject=520.

Even among formal workers, a significant portion will not be able to contribute to both the BPJS-JP and the BPJS-JHT schemes. Seventeen per cent of formal employees are working in small or micro enterprises and do not contribute to the BPJS-JP scheme.

Expected replacement rates vary across different types of workers. Civil servants can expect very high replacement rates. This is mainly driven by an expected replacement rate of 80% from the DB pension plan after 32 years of contributions. In addition, public servants also contribute to a DC scheme, resulting in an additional replacement rate for public servants of 11.6% for males and 10.0% for females from Taspen-THT assuming 40 years of contributions.

Expected replacement rates are reasonable for workers in medium and large enterprises, but only when assuming an unrealistically optimistic scenario, and replacement rates for other workers are lower. The maximum replacement rates for average-earning private sector employees are 33.1% from the BPJS-JP and 20.4% from the BPJS-JHT, for a total expected replacement rate of 53.5% for employees covered by both schemes. Because of their longer life expectancies, women have a lower total replacement rate of 50.6% (OECD, 2023[3]). These figures represent a maximum because this calculation assumes that an employee enters the labour market today and contributes for a full career to the age of 65. The benefits from the BPJS-JP plan are subject to a minimum and maximum amount of IDR 350 700 and IDR 4 207 200, respectively, meaning that the lowest-income employees will receive higher replacement rates, and highest-income employees will have a lower one. The minimum pension represented 12.3% of the gross average wage in 2020 (OECD, 2022[4]). However, the lower threshold is not currently triggered for workers earning at least 50% of average earnings, and the higher threshold is just triggered for those earning 200% of average earnings (OECD, 2023[3]). Employees of small and micro enterprises, who cannot contribute to the BPJS-JP, can expect a much lower maximum replacement rate of only 20.4% for men and 17.5% for women coming from the BPJS-JHT.

The Indonesian Ministry of Finance calculates a replacement rate from these schemes based on a more realistic scenario of 32 years of service, which results in lower replacement rates. Under this assumption replacement rates for private sector employees are 14.5% from the BPJS-JP and 12.6% from the BPJS-JHT (Kementerian Keuangan Republik Indonesia, 2024[5]). However, potential replacement rates for civil servants remain high, because workers can receive the maximum replacement rate from the DB scheme after 32 years of contributions.

Replacement rates for private sector workers should increase over time as the schemes mature and people contribute to the system for longer periods of time. Meanwhile, actual maximum replacement rates will be lower than the full potential as the BPJS schemes have only been in operation since 2015. The first worker that will be able to contribute for 40 years will not retire until 2055. Further, those retiring before 2030 will not reach 15 years of contributions and therefore will not receive any lifetime income from the BPJS-JP scheme, but will instead receive a lump sum.

However, even when the system is mature, actual replacement rates are likely to be below the maximum potential because many people tend to have short active lives and large rates of informality. Table 1.4 summarises the maximum replacement rates from the mandatory schemes for different types of workers based on both the OECD's methodology and the estimates of the Ministry of Finance that assumes a shorter contribution period.

## Table 1.4. Maximum replacement rates from publicly-managed pension schemes

| Type of Worker | Maximum replacement rate for **males** from publicly-managed schemes (OECD) | Maximum replacement rate for **females** from publicly-managed schemes (OECD) | Maximum replacement rate from publicly-managed schemes (MoF)* |
|---|---|---|---|
| Public servant | 91.6% | 90.0% | 87.2% |
| Large/medium enterprise | 53.5% | 50.6% | 27.4% |
| Small enterprise | 20.4% | 17.5% | 12.6% |
| Micro enterprise | 20.4% | 17.5% | 12.6% |
| Informal | 7.2% | 6.1% | 1.6% |

Note: *Assumes 32 years of contributions compared to 43 years for OECD calculations.
Source: OECD (2023[3]), Pensions at a Glance 2023: OECD and G20 Indicators, https://www.oecd.org/content/dam/oecd/en/publications/reports/2023/12/pensions-at-a-glance-2023_4757bf20/678055dd-en.pdf; Kementerian Keuangan Republik Indonesia (2024[5]) and OECD approximations.

Additionally, the indexation of the cap on benefits for the BPJS-JP scheme presents a risk that this scheme will not deliver the same level of benefits in the future. While the cap on benefits is not currently restrictive, going forward it will be indexed to prices. However, individuals contribute as a percentage of their wage, and if wages grow faster than prices the cap could become more restrictive. The World Bank estimates that if wages grow at 5% and inflation at 2%, everyone earning an average wage and over would be subject to the cap on benefits by 2060, and the benefits received would no longer have much of a link to the contributions made (Holmemo et al., 2020[6]).

### *1.1.2. Retirement ages*

Retirement ages differ across the system leading to individuals retire at the earliest possible age and resulting in more years of retirement that retirement savings will need to finance. The normal retirement age for the BPJS-JP plans is gradually increasing from 58 in 2022 to 65 in 2043. However, the retirement age for the BPJS-JHT is not increasing in parallel. As a result, most people are still retiring earlier at the age of 56.

People retiring at 56 will have to finance a much longer period in retirement. In 2019, life expectancy at age 56 was 20.7 years, compared to 14.2 years at age 65 (United Nations, 2022[7]). However, the maximum replacement rates shown in Table 1.4 assume a retirement age of 65 in 2065, when life expectancy at age 65 is projected to be 17.3 years (United Nations, 2022[7]).[2] So not only do retirees need to finance a retirement period longer than that estimated for the calculations in Table 1.4 if retiring at age 56, people retiring today will have saved in the BPJS-JHT system for less than 10 years, instead of the 43 years of savings assumed. Replacement rates will therefore be much lower than the estimated maximums.

### *1.1.3. Allowed payout options*

The BPJS-JP scheme will only provide members with income in retirement when the system becomes more mature. Individuals will have to have contributed for 15 years before receiving lifetime payments from the BPJS-JP scheme. Those who have contributed for a shorter period, which includes those retiring before 2030, will receive their benefits as a lump sum.

Benefits from the BPJS-JHT plan are paid as a lump sum and not as a retirement income. Additionally, it is very easy for members to withdraw their money before retirement, as the current rules allow for full withdrawals when changing jobs after only five years of contributions. Between 2016 and 2018, an average of 1.5 million people per month withdrew their savings from the JHT because they left their job, which was the main reason for withdrawals from the scheme. A smaller proportion withdraw because of job-loss (as opposed to resignation), and around the same amount was withdrawn when a member reached retirement age (Ministry of Finance, 2024[8]).

The allowed timing for withdrawals from voluntary plans is more restrictive. Individuals can only take benefits from voluntary occupational funds five years before the normal retirement age of 55. Prior to Law 4/2023, employees could take benefits ten years from the retirement age established by their employer.

Additionally, there are more restrictions around taking lump sums from voluntary plans. For voluntary DPPK DB plans, benefits can be paid as a lump sum if the lifetime income benefits are less than IDR 1.6 million per month or if the present value of benefits calculated at retirement is less than IDR 500 million. Otherwise, members can take only 20% of their benefits as a lump sum, with the rest taken as periodic payments paid by the pension fund or as a life annuity with a minimum duration of ten years from a life insurance company.

For voluntary DC plans (DPPK and DPLK), benefits can be paid as a lump sum if savings are less than IDR 500 million. Otherwise, members can take only 20% of their benefits as a lump sum, with the rest taken as a periodic payment with a minimum duration of ten years, paid by the pension fund as a drawdown or as an annuity by a life insurance company. Members of DPLK plans may also take their savings as a lump sum if they can prove financial hardship, have been diagnosed with a critical illness, have changed their Indonesian nationality, or are a foreign citizen no longer working in Indonesia.

Taxation of pensions is largely in line with international practice, though the taxation of withdrawals tends to favour lump sums over periodic payments. Contributions to voluntary pension funds and any earned investment income are tax exempt, while withdrawals are subject to taxation. There are no limits to the tax-deductibility of contributions.

## 1.2. Protection gaps arising from availability

While the rules of the system provide a minimum availability of pension schemes to accumulate retirement benefits, the availability of voluntary occupational schemes may be more limited. In addition, lifetime income vehicles are not always available for the decumulation of retirement savings.

### *1.2.1. Accumulation of retirement benefits*

All individuals in Indonesia have a pension plan available to them. The introduction of the BPJS-JHT scheme in 2015 ensured that all workers can access a retirement savings scheme. In addition, any individual can access a personal retirement savings plan provided by a financial institution regardless of their employment status. There are currently 25 life insurers and banks offering DC pension plans, and now asset managers are also allowed to offer plans (OJK, 2024[9]).

Employers commonly make voluntary occupational pension plans. In 2015, 62% of companies provided an occupational pension plan, with 20% of these providing DB plans and 83% providing DC plans. Employer contribution rates to these plans are normally around 6-8% of salaries. While employee contributions are normally not required, if they are they are usually around 3% (Rosedewayani, 2017[10]).

However, since the introduction of the mandatory BPJS schemes, there has been a trend to close employer pension plans. Indonesia decided not to allow employees to opt-out of participating in the mandatory scheme if their employer pension plan offered better benefits. As a result, many companies closed their plans and contributions went instead to the BPJS schemes. The number of DB employer funds (DPPK PPMP) decreased from 164 in 2018 to 138 in 2023, and the number of DC employer funds (DPPK PPIP) decreased from 44 to 36 (OJK, 2024[9]; OJK, 2022[11]). In 2022, 96 DPPK closed to new members. Employers can also convert their DB plans to DC plans with the agreement of employees. The number of DPLK funds have remained more steady, with 25 funds in 2023 (OJK, 2024[9]). Some stakeholders are concerned that the proposal to introduce additional mandatory contributions for those with higher incomes could lead to further closures because there will be less capacity for voluntary savings.

### *1.2.2. Decumulation of retirement benefits*

Life insurance companies generally do not offer products or vehicles paying lifetime incomes. The products previously offered allowed individuals to surrender their product and receive a cash value rather than continuing to receive payments for life. The new legislation therefore introduced the requirement for the payout of retirement savings to be over at least ten years to ensure these products provide a regular income.

## 1.3. Protection gaps arising from uptake

Even though individuals may have access to pension plans, they still may not make use of the vehicles available to save for their retirement. A lack of uptake of retirement savings can lead to lower-than-expected coverage. Low levels of voluntary savings also lead to lower replacement rates, even for those contributing to a plan.

### *1.3.1. Coverage*

A large proportion of formal workers do not contribute to a pension plan, despite it being mandatory. There were 21.6 million members of mandatory pension schemes (excluding military) in 2024, representing around 11% of the population aged 15 to 65, and around 15% of the labour force (OJK, 2024[12]). Only around 38% of formal workers participate in a mandatory pension programme, implying a non-compliance rate of 62%.

Women are less likely to participate in a BPJS scheme, though this is simply reflective of their participation in the labour market. Women make up around one third of active members in both the BPJS-JP and BPJS-JHT schemes, but they also make up around one third of the formal labour market.

Voluntary participation in the BPJS scheme is extremely low. Only around 0.5% of informal workers participate in the BPJS-JHT scheme.

Participation and coverage of occupational and personal plans is also very low. There were around 1.25 million participants in DPPK in 2024, or around 3% of the employees of large and medium enterprises.[3] There were around 3 million participants in DPLK plans in 2024, representing around 2% of the total workforce.[4]

### *1.3.2. Contributions*

Average income levels vary widely across different population groups, which can also determine to what extent individuals have the capacity to contribute to pension plans after meeting basic expenditure needs. The average monthly net income of regular employees as of August 2023 was IDR 3 178 227. The average net income of the self-employed was 63% that of regular employees. The average net income of informal workers was less than 50% of the net income of regular employees (BPS-Statistics Indonesia, 2024[13]).

Comparing expenditure to income can indicate the capacity for individuals to save additional sums for their retirement. The average monthly expenditure on food in all of Indonesia was IDR 711 282 in 2023, or 22% of the average net monthly income of a regular employee, and nearly 50% of total consumption, including non-food (BPS-Statistics Indonesia, 2024[13]). This implies that average employees may have some additional capacity to save more.

## 1.4. Additional challenges faced by the asset-backed pension system in Indonesia

The Indonesian pension system faces three additional key challenges that will be important to address to achieve desired retirement outcomes. These challenges relate to the investment of pension funds, their solvency and sustainability, and the harmonisation and complementarity of the system.

### *1.4.1. Investment in appropriate long-term strategies for financing retirement*

The mandatory BPJS schemes and the voluntary occupational schemes both face challenges with respect to implementing appropriate long-term investment strategies to finance retirement. For the BPJS-JHT scheme, the rules in place impede investment in growth assets and assets with a longer duration, and there is a lack of transparency around investment performance. The investment of voluntary occupational schemes lacks rules and incentives to facilitate and encourage diversified investment strategies. For both types of schemes, the governance framework does not require sufficient technical and investment knowledge to develop and supervise an appropriate investment strategy.

### *BPJS's investment*

The asset allocation of the pension funds managed by the BPJS in 2022 was heavily weighted towards fixed income instruments and deposits. In addition, most assets are also of short maturities (Kementerian Keuangan Republik Indonesia, 2024[5]). Over 50% of the portfolio for the JHT scheme is invested in government bonds and other bonds, with an additional 17% invested in Islamic Bonds. Another 12% of the portfolio is invested in deposits, leaving only 18.5% of the portfolio invested in other investments including mutual funds and equities. Asset allocations for the JP scheme are slightly more tilted towards fixed income and deposits, with 65% invested in government bonds, 12% invested in Islamic Bonds, 8% in deposits, leaving around 15% for other investments. The composition of assets for the JHT and JP schemes in 2022 is shown in Figure 1.2.

**Figure 1.2. Asset allocations for the BJPS schemes, 2022**

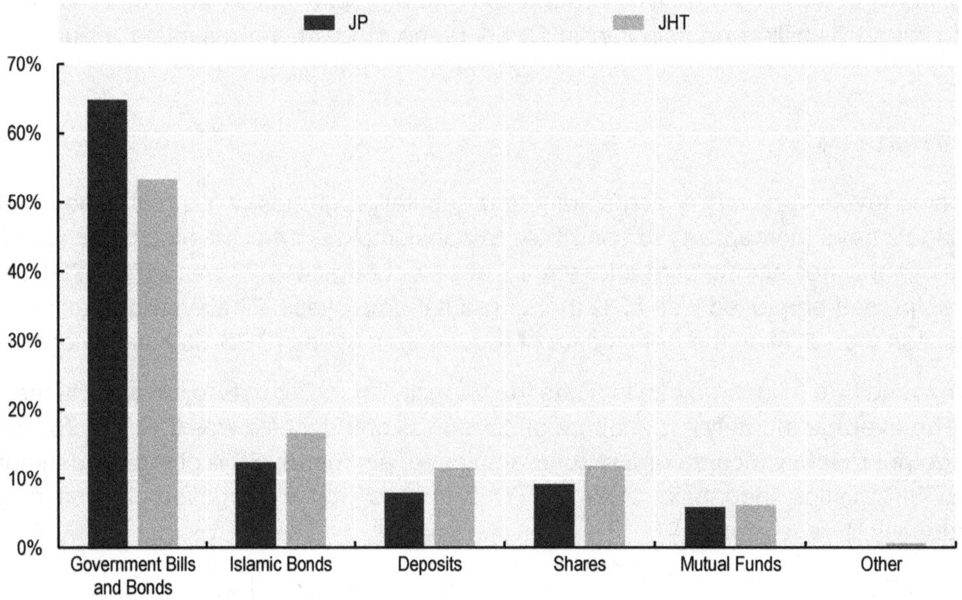


Source: OJK (2022[14]), Indonesia's Social Security Statistics.

One reason for the concentration of fixed income instruments in the BPJS's investment strategy has been an anti-corruption law which effectively prevented investment managers of public institutions from selling any assets that had declined in value, and thereby realise the investment losses, because the auditors would be obliged to report this as a potential crime (the 'cut loss' problem). Investing primarily in short-term fixed-income securities minimised the potential need to sell at a loss, thereby mitigating the liability that the investment managers could face. The legislation passed in 2023 now explicitly allows investment managers to realise investment losses, so going forward they should have more flexibility to adjust their portfolio and asset allocations.

Another impediment to investing in longer-duration assets is the volume of early withdrawals from the JHT plan. Individuals are able to withdraw all of their assets from the scheme when they change jobs once they have made five years of contributions. In 2018, withdrawals from the JHT for all reasons totalled IDR 22.3 trillion, representing just under half the amount of contributions received that year. However, the gap between withdrawals and contributions has been shrinking rapidly over time. In 2022, withdrawals from the JHT plan represented over three-quarters of the contributions coming in (OJK, 2022[14]). This implies that contributions may not be sufficient to cover withdrawals in the near future, and eventually assets may need to be sold to cover liquidity needs.

While the asset allocation for the JHT scheme seems overly conservative and under-diversified for the long-term objective of financing retirement, their investment returns are not readily available. The BPJS does not report its investment performance, but only the total change in asset values, which makes it difficult to measure and assess the investment and asset allocation decisions they make.

To address this problem, the government is revising regulation relating to the asset and liability management of the BPJS, including rules on assessing performance using benchmarks weighted by asset class.

Nevertheless, moving towards better matching the duration of investments with the long-term horizon to invest for retirement remains a challenge due to a lack of long-term investment opportunities in the market, and there are few instruments available for funds to hedge retirement-income related risks.

Another challenge to implementing adequate long-term investment strategies is a lack of sufficient expertise in the governing body of the schemes. The governing body of the BPJS is made up of seven board members. Two are appointed by the government, one each from the Ministry of Labour and the Ministry of Finance. There are also two representatives each from the unions and employers, along with a single independent expert. The government must put 10 candidates forward to Parliament for the non-government representatives. The Parliament then chooses 5 candidates to appoint of these 10 . The only candidate necessarily having a technical knowledge of pensions is the independent expert. In practice, the body has a memorandum of understanding with OJK to oversee some financial aspects of the BPJS pension funds, but OJK does not have any power to intervene as a supervisor (The World Bank Group, 2024[15]).

### *Voluntary occupational pension funds' investment*

The rules and incentives in place have contributed to a significant lack of diversification of pension funds' investment strategies. They deter voluntary occupational pension funds from investing in an appropriate long-term strategy to finance retirement. The investment limits are a key driver of this. Voluntary pension funds must invest a minimum of 30% in Indonesian government bonds, and are effectively not allowed to invest abroad.

In addition to a lack of diversification, the asset allocations of voluntary pension funds also tend to be very conservative, even though domestic investment in equities is not overly restrictive. The employer pension funds (DPPKs) follow similar asset allocations as the BPJS, with just over 60% of assets allocated to bills and bonds, and around 10% in cash and deposits, leaving around 30% for other investments, including 10% investment in equities by DPPK DB plans and 15% by DPPK DC plans. However, pension funds managed by financial institutions (DPLKs) are significantly more conservative in their investment. On average in 2023, these funds invested over 50% in cash and deposits, 40% in bills and bonds, and only 10% in other investments, of which only 2% in equities (Figure 1.3).

**Figure 1.3. Allocation of assets earmarked for retirement in selected asset classes and investment vehicles in Indonesia and OECD countries, 2023**

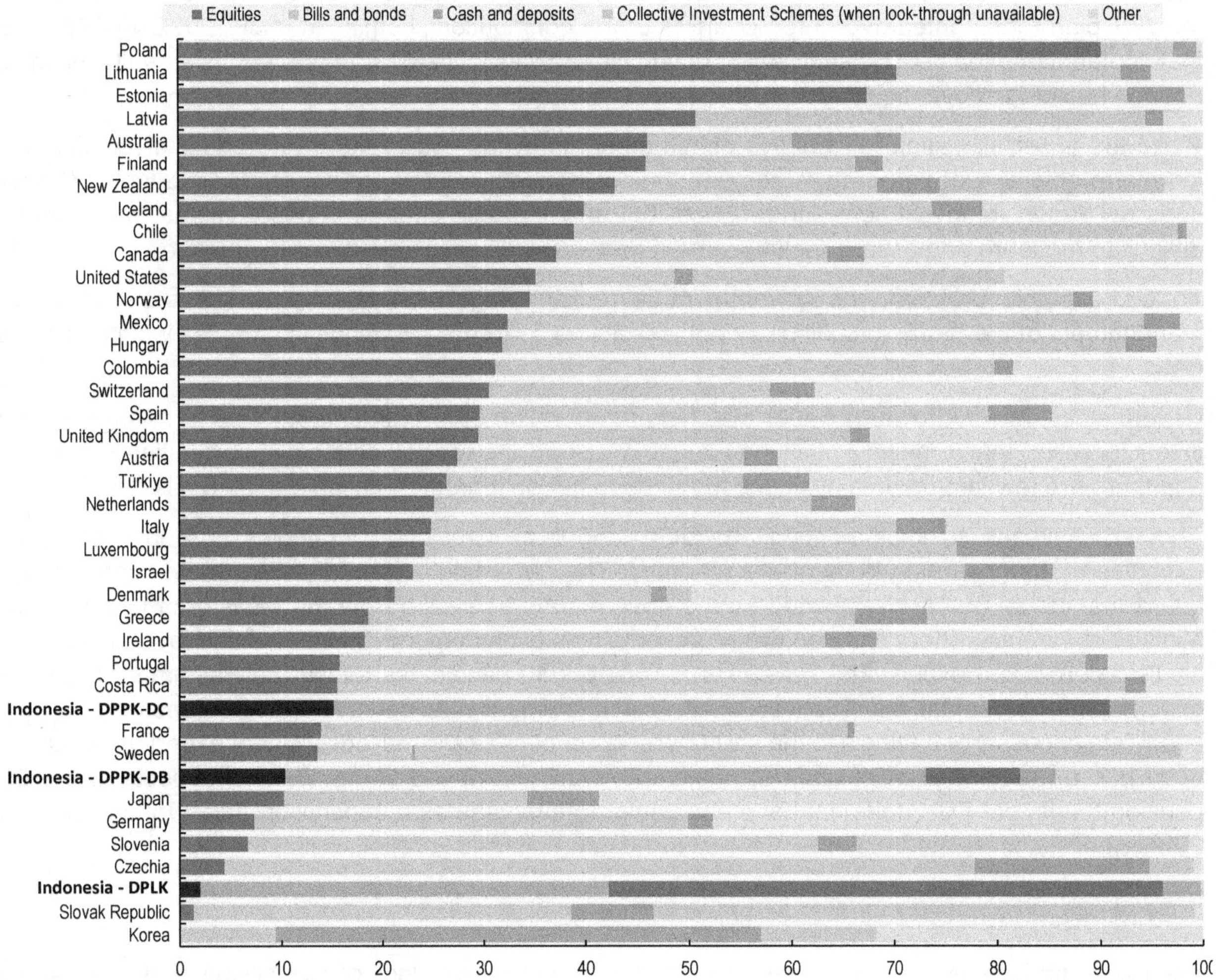


Source: OECD (2024[16]), Pension Markets in Focus 2024, https://www.oecd.org/en/publications/pension-markets-in-focus-2024_b11473d3-en.html.

Nevertheless, DPLKs have managed to achieve similar real investment returns as DC DPPKs, at around 2.5% on average over the last decade, though this is behind the 3.8% return achieved by the DB DPPKs (Figure 1.4). While these returns compare positively to the performance of pension fund investments in OECD jurisdictions, this is mainly driven by the relatively high yield that Indonesian government bonds have enjoyed over the last decade.

**Figure 1.4. Geometric average annual real investment rates of return, in Indonesia and other jurisdictions, between Dec 2012 and Dec 2022**

In %

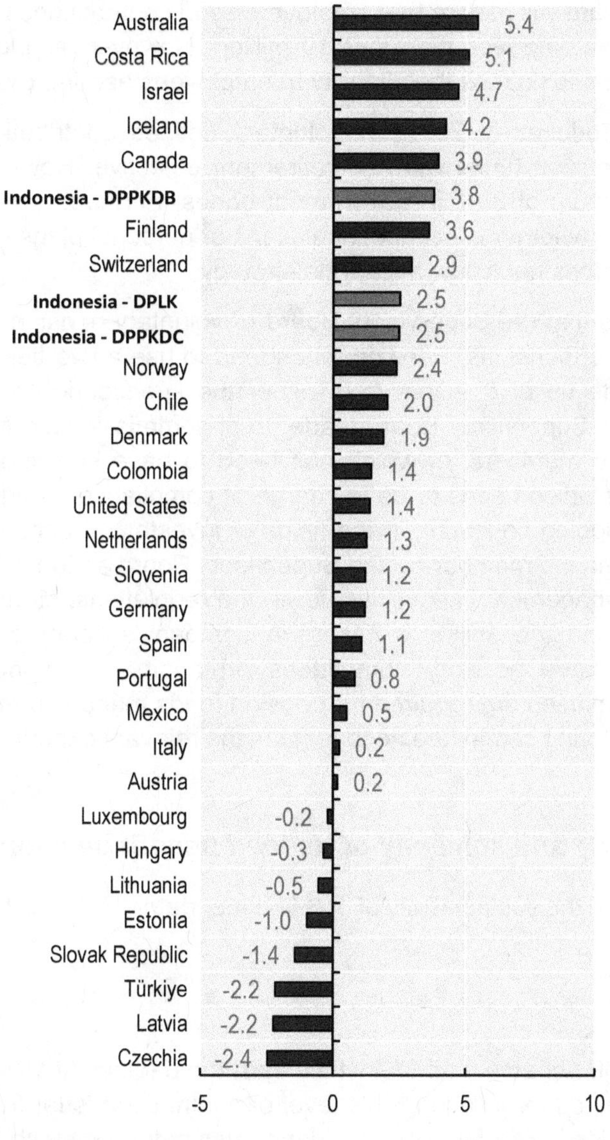


Note: Data for Australia are from June to June.

Source: OJK and OECD (2023[17]), Pension Markets in Focus 2023, https://www.oecd.org/en/publications/pension-markets-in-focus-2023_28970baf-en.html.

A key driver in the conservatism of the investment strategies of voluntary occupational pension funds is the requirement for firms to pay a severance payment to employees leaving their employment due to retirement, death or disability. Employers must recognise the liability of severance payments owed to their employees on their balance sheet. While there is no requirement for these liabilities to be funded, employers offering pension plans to their employees can use the assets from those plans to offset their severance liability on their balance sheet. In addition, employers funding their severance liability through pension funds can enjoy tax-deductible contributions, and benefits are subject to a lower pension tax. Employers can therefore make the same contributions to a pension plan as they would have had to make directly to finance severance benefits for employees, but enjoy additional tax benefits. The investment objective is therefore not to maximise retirement outcomes for their employees, but rather to invest with as little risk as possible to be sure that their contributions to finance the severance benefit will not lose value.

In part to address this problem, the recent legislation reduced the severance benefits that employees are entitled to, and going forward will require that employers send contributions to the JHT scheme to fund the liabilities for employees earning less than IDR 10 million. However, employers will still be able to use occupational pension funds to finance their liability to employees earning over this amount.

Lifecycle funds were introduced in 2017 for voluntary defined contribution plans to better align the investment strategy of pension funds with the retirement objective. However, these strategies are still required to invest a minimum of 30% in government bonds. Furthermore, they are only mandatory for individuals' contributions – whether in occupational plans or personal plans – and therefore the majority of pension fund investment does not follow a lifecycle strategy.

An additional challenge is that the Supervisory Board of voluntary pension funds is not required to have any technical knowledge of pensions. Pension funds tend to use a two-tier governance system, with the Management Board made up of directors from either the sponsoring employer or the financial entity managing the fund, and a Supervisory Board made up of commissioners. Management Boards must be comprised of at least two members, of which half need to have knowledge in investment and/or risk management, and one of which needs to be in charge of compliance. In addition, there is a requirement for members to follow ongoing education in the fields of investment, accounting, risk management, and actuarial science. However, the members of the Supervisory Board are only required to have more general knowledge relating to management capabilities, laws and regulations, strategic management and sound business development, and the ability to assess a company's financial situation. Nevertheless, the Supervisory Board can have advisory committees on audit, risk monitoring, and nomination and remuneration. Such committees are required for pension funds managing more than IDR 100 billion, and members of the risk monitoring committee need to have the relevant experience. There are no committees on investment, however.

### *1.4.2. The sustainability and solvency of defined benefit pension schemes*

There are concerns around the sustainability of both the mandatory BPJS-JP DB scheme and the voluntary DPPK DB schemes.

#### *Sustainability of the BPJS-JP DB scheme*

The contributions to the JP scheme total 3%, which earn the participant 1% of their salary paid each year for life in retirement, adjusted for inflation. This level of contribution is far from being sufficient to finance the level of benefit promised. The Ministry of Finance estimates that with this level of contribution, the scheme will have no more invested assets by around 2070 (Kementerian Keuangan Republik Indonesia, 2024[5]). They estimate an actuarially fair contribution rate closer to 5% assuming 30 years of service, but even increasing contributions to this level now will eventually result in deficits as the scheme is already underfunded. By law, the contribution rate to the scheme must be reviewed every three years, but so far there have been no changes since the inception of the scheme.

#### *Sustainability of the DPPK DB schemes*

There are insufficient guardrails in place to ensure the sustainability of the occupational DPPK DB pension schemes. While employers are required to finance any funding deficit of their DB schemes, the requirements around how the deficit is measured are very flexible. Funding can be calculated either through a solvency termination measure or an ongoing valuation measure. The assumptions on which funding calculations are based are also not subject to rigorous oversight.

One assumption that may be problematic is the discount rate used to value the defined benefit pension liabilities. The average interest rate used for valuations is 8%, and this ranges between 5% and 10%. Although the simple average of returns of these funds over the last decade has been 8%, as shown in Figure 1.5, around one-third of the funds use an interest rate above 8% (OJK, 2022[11]). In reality, many DB plans therefore have a worse funding position than they actually report.

**Figure 1.5. Annual investment returns by type of pension fund**

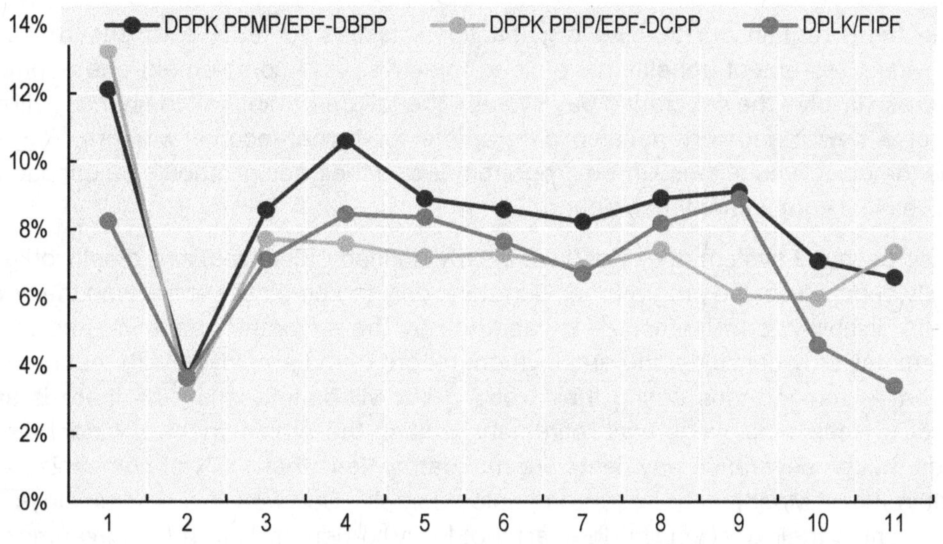


Source: OJK (2022[11]), Statistik Dana Pensiun 2022, https://ojk.go.id/id/kanal/iknb/data-dan-statistik/dana-pensiun/Documents/Pages/Buku-Statistik-Dana-Pensiun-2022/Buku%20Statistik%20Dana%20Pensiun%202022.pdf.

There are also no formal requirements for the mortality assumptions used to value liabilities. In practice, pension funds usually adjust standard mortality tables to reflect the mortality of the plan members, and assumptions usually account for future mortality improvements.

To add to the potential underfunding of DB plans, many pension funds have contributions that are receivable and have not yet been paid by employers. This means that the funding ratio calculation does not necessarily reflect the actual assets invested, which would also result in overstating the funding position of these plans.

In addition, the high proportion of investments in government bonds presents increased exposure to concentration risk. If there was a default on those obligations, it could trigger a solvency problem for all the DB pension schemes.

### *1.4.3. The complementarity of the different components of the system*

The harmonisation of the pension system is a key priority of the government and an objective of many of the reforms being carried out. There has already been significant progress in streamlining the organisation of the system. Before 2014, the institutional framework for the management of social benefits was fragmented. The reorganisation of the system consolidated the various institutions into two: BPJS Employment (BPJS Ketenagakerjaan) that manages employment-related benefits, and BPJS Kesehatan that manages health-related benefits. BPJS Employment now manages the two mandatory pension schemes for private sector employees, the JP and the JHT. It registers members, collects contributions, administers benefits and manages the investment of assets.

The recent Law 4/2023 included several measures that intend to improve the efficiency and harmonisation of the pension system. A single employer pension fund (DPPK) may now manage both a DB plan and a DC plan, which should allow the funds to better optimise operational costs. The law also now requires DC pension funds to manage the transition from accumulation of retirement savings to the payout of savings in retirement, either by providing a programmed withdrawal or transferring the assets to an insurance company to purchase an annuity, which should facilitate members' transition to retirement. The law also standardised the allowed retirement ages for occupational pension plans, which previously varied widely across plans. Now, the minimum retirement age in these plans is 55, and early retirement cannot be earlier than 5 years before the normal early retirement age in the system.

Nevertheless, there remain outstanding organisational issues to resolve to ensure that the different schemes providing retirement benefits have clear objectives and complement one another. Three main issues to address involve the severance pay system, the failure of the JHT to finance retirement, and the introduction of a new mandatory pension programme for higher-income workers. Regulations should clearly define the objectives of these three programmes and their design should be conducive to achieving those objectives in a complementary manner.

The severance payment system does not have clearly defined objectives, and most workers are not able to substantially benefit from the programme. Currently, only the employer at the time the benefit is claimed – i.e. at death, disability, or retirement – is liable to pay the severance benefits, and the calculation of benefit entitlements only considers the employment record of the employee with that employer. As such, people who have changed jobs during their working life will benefit less, and there is an incentive for employers not to keep employees until retirement, putting the employment of older workers at risk. In addition, even though severance payments are mandatory, less than 20% of companies actually comply with the requirement. Mostly only large companies comply. So even if a worker stays with the same employer throughout their working life, they are not likely to benefit from a full severance payment. The Law 6/2023 reduced benefits paid under the severance system, which comprised of a formula accounting for severance pay, service pay, and additional compensation amounting to 15% of the other amounts. Previously, benefits were equivalent in the case of death or retirement, and the service allowance for disability was doubled. Now, the compensation pay has been eliminated, the additional service compensation in the case of disability removed, and the severance pay in the case of retirement reduced. The authorities are considering additional reforms that would require employers to pre-finance severance liabilities through the JHT scheme instead of through a DPPK or DPLK for those earning less than IDR 10 million.[5] However, the purpose of the severance system in providing benefits for retirement remains unclear, and the incentives to use occupational pension funds to finance the severance liabilities for higher earners remain.

Another challenge relates to the failure of the BPJS-JHT scheme to fulfil any objective relating to financing retirement benefits. The majority of assets are withdrawn when members change or lose their job, and only a small fraction of assets are withdrawn at retirement. The light blue bars in Figure 1.6 shows this. To address this, the authorities are separating savings in the JHT scheme into two accounts: one reserved to finance retirement, and another that can be used as emergency savings in the case of health problems, illness, unemployment, or alternatively for the purchase of a first home.

**Figure 1.6. Withdrawals from the BPJS-JHT scheme, in trillion IDR**

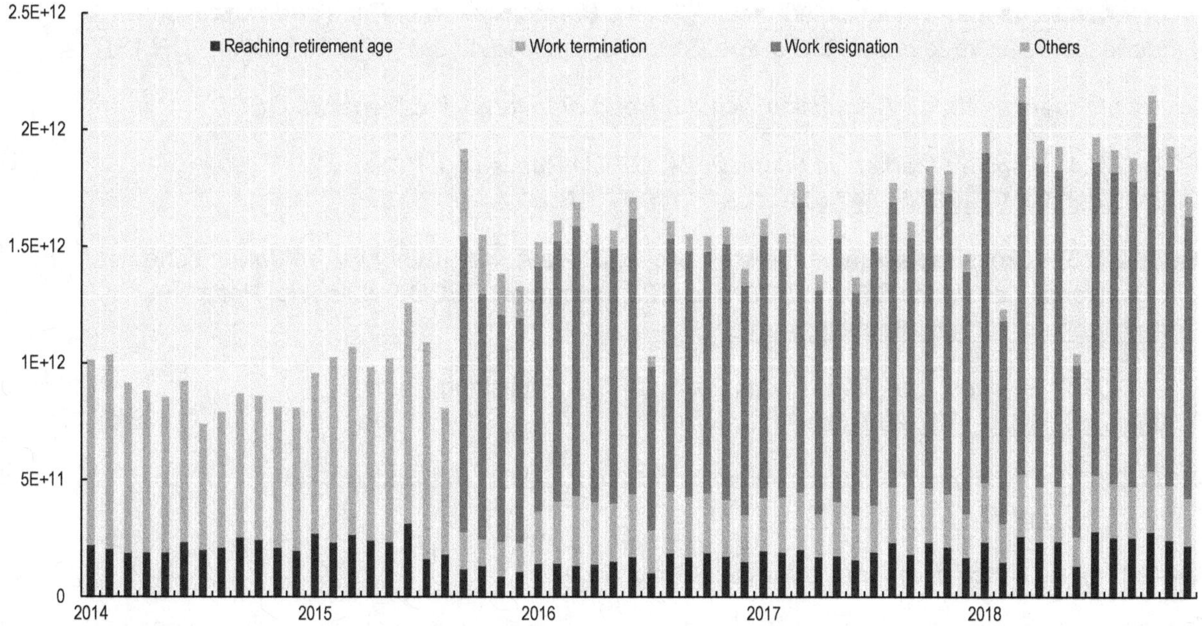


Source: Kementerian Keuangan Republik Indonesia (2024[5]).

Finally, the Indonesian authorities have also introduced a new requirement for additional mandatory contributions to a DC scheme for employees earning more than IDR 10 million per month.[5] Which institution will manage these contributions is not yet clear. Investing the additional contributions in the JHT scheme is one option, however the BPJS only has a legal mandate to manage the basic pension benefits for the population, and not the supplementary benefits, so depending on the interpretation of their mandate, their management of additional contributions could require changes in legislation. The other option would be for the private pension funds to manage the additional contributions.

Regardless of the solution chosen to manage these additional contributions, this new requirement will only impact about 5% of the working population. Therefore, while it will contribute to the goal of increasing replacement rates from the pension system, it will only do so for a small minority of the population who are already better off financially and who already contribute more to the system. Additionally, providers of pension funds are concerned that an increase in mandatory contributions will reduce the appetite for voluntary savings in occupational pension plans and exacerbate the trend to close plans offered by employers.

## References


BPS-Statistics Indonesia (2024), *Income and Consumption Database*, https://www.bps.go.id/en/statistics-table?subject=523. [13]

BPS-Statistics Indonesia (2023), *Labour Statistics*, https://www.bps.go.id/en/statistics-table?subject=520 (accessed on June 2024). [2]

Holmemo, C. et al. (2020), *Investing in People: Social protection for Indonesia's 2020 vision*, The Wold Bank, https://documents1.worldbank.org/curated/en/384621587010378649/pdf/Main-Report.pdf. [6]

ILO (2025), *ILO Modelled Estimates and Projections database*, http://ilostat.ilo.org/data. [1]

Kementerian Keuangan Republik Indonesia (2024), *Harmonization of Pension Programs in Indonesia: Initiative to Improve Old-age Protection and Advanceing Public Welfar - DRAFT*. [5]

Ministry of Finance (2024), *Discussion with the Head of Insurance & Pension, OECD*. [8]

OECD (2024), *Pension Markets in Focus 2024*, OECD Publishing, Paris, https://doi.org/10.1787/b11473d3-en. [16]

OECD (2023), "Gross replacement rates: Public vs. Private, Mandatory vs. Voluntary schemes", in *Pensions at a Glance 2023: OECD and G20 Indicators*, OECD Publishing, Paris, https://doi.org/10.1787/6ee56185-en. [3]

OECD (2023), *Pension Markets in Focus 2023*, OECD Publishing, Paris, https://doi.org/10.1787/28970baf-en. [17]

OECD (2022), *Pensions at a Glance Asia/Pacific 2022*, OECD Publishing, Paris, https://doi.org/10.1787/2c555ff8-en. [4]

OJK (2024), *A Glance of Indonesia Pension Program*. [9]

OJK (2024), *Roadmap for the development & strengthening of Indonesia pension fund 2024-2028*. [12]

OJK (2022), *Indonesia's Social Security Statistics*. [14]

OJK (2022), *Statistik Dana Pensiun 2022*, https://ojk.go.id/id/kanal/iknb/data-dan-statistik/dana-pensiun/Documents/Pages/Buku-Statistik-Dana-Pensiun-2022/Buku%20Statistik%20Dana%20Pensiun%202022.pdf. [11]

Rosedewayani, S. (2017), *Fiscal and other incentives for pension and saving schemes in Indonesia*, https://www.ojk.go.id/id/kanal/iknb/berita-dan-kegiatan/info-terkini/Documents/Pages/OJK-dan-World-Bank-Gelar-Indonesia-Pension-Conference/Session3_Pension%20Day_Fiscal%20and%20Other%20Incentive_Santhi%20Devi%20WTW_v4.pdf. [10]

The World Bank Group (2024), *Indonesia Financial Sector Assessment Program Technical Note: Long term finance and capital market development*. [15]

United Nations (2022), *World Population Prospects*, http://population.un.org/wpp/. [7]


## Notes

[1] This is the same definition of informality than in Latin American countries. It means that the self-employed are classified as informal workers. This is not the case in North America, Europe or Japan.

[2] Life expectancy figures do not account for future expected mortality improvements, so the average amount of time that an individual can expect to be in retirement is actually longer.

[3] Removing participants in Asabri and Taspen, who have around 4.8 million members.

[4] Based on employment statistics from 2022. The breakdown of participants in occupational and personal DPLK plans is not available.

[5] This amount is still under discussion.

# 2 Policy options to address the protection gaps and challenges for the asset-backed pension system

This chapter discusses the various measures that the Indonesian authorities have taken to address the challenges relating to retirement savings described and proposes additional measures that they could consider to improve retirement outcomes, drawing on OECD guidelines and international good practices.

Indonesia could consider numerous measures to close protection gaps and address the challenges it faces relating to investment, sustainability and the harmonisation and complementarity of the pension system. This chapter discusses the various measures that the Indonesian authorities have taken to address the challenges relating to retirement savings described and proposes additional measures that they could consider to improve retirement outcomes, drawing on OECD guidelines and international good practices.

## 2.1. Ensure the rules of the pension system to allow individuals to accumulate adequate retirement savings

The introduction of the mandatory pension schemes for private sector workers in 2015 was a significant step towards improving access to pension schemes for the Indonesian population. Nevertheless, workers who are not employed in large or medium sized enterprises remain underserved, as they generally do not contribute to the BPJS-JP scheme and informal workers have lower contribution rates to the BPJS-JHT scheme.

The Indonesian authorities have taken several measures to increase contributions and replacement rates, but these are primarily focused on those who already contribute more to the system because of their employment status or salary. Voluntary schemes are primarily offered in large and medium sized companies, whose employees are also mandated to contribute to the BPJS-JP scheme. The government is also introducing a new mandatory pension programme, but this will be targeted at those with higher earnings so will not improve the situation for middle- to lower-income workers, who generally have fewer opportunities to access and contribute to a retirement savings scheme.

The normal retirement age is not harmonised across the mandatory publicly-provided pension schemes for private sector workers. While the retirement age for the BPJS-JP scheme is gradually increasing to age 65, that for the BPJS-JHT scheme remains 56. As such, individuals tend to retire at the earliest possible age, at 56. Replacement rates from the yet-to-mature publicly-provided schemes are currently low, and they will not be able to finance a retirement of over 20 years with so few years of contributions.

However, the government has already taken measures to harmonise the retirement ages for voluntary occupational pension plans. The minimum pension age that voluntary schemes can offer is now five years before the normal retirement age of 55. This should increase the retirement savings accumulated in voluntary schemes.

The government has also taken steps to introduce more flexibility in how people receive payouts from voluntary pension plans. Since 2023, periodic payouts from both DB and DC plans can be paid over a minimum of ten years rather than for life, and there are additional limits around how lump sums can be taken. While full lump-sums are not always allowed for voluntary plans, lump-sums tend to be taxed more favourably than annuities.

Nevertheless, the BPJS-JHT scheme continues to pay out only lump-sums, and drawdowns or annuities from this plan are not available.

The Indonesian authorities could consider several measures to improve the rules of the system to deliver better retirement outcomes. Some potential options to improve access to retirement savings schemes would be to align the contribution rates across different types of workers, harmonise the schemes between public and private sector workers, and to reformulate the cap on benefits from the BPJS-JP scheme. Publicly-provided schemes could encourage later retirement by harmonising the retirement ages. The rules around the payout options available could be more coherent with the intended role of the different components of the pension system by limiting payout options for the BPJS-JHT scheme before retirement and remaining neutral with respect to the taxation of the different payout options.

### 2.1.1. Align contribution rates across different types of workers

Private sector workers who are not required to contribute to the BPJS-JP scheme miss out on benefits coming from the additional 3% contribution made to the scheme for employees of medium and large enterprises. In addition, this population is not likely to have access to an occupational pension plan. Furthermore, informal workers are only allowed to contribute 2% to the BPJS-JHT scheme, whereas formal employees benefit from an additional contribution of 3.7% from their employer. The only option for those wishing to save more for their retirement is to save in a personal plan offered by a financial institution, which is likely to incur higher fees.

The OECD recommends aligning contribution rates across all types of workers (OECD, 2019[1]). Most OECD countries do not differentiate contribution caps by type of worker for asset-backed pension plans. Nevertheless, eight OECD countries have higher contribution caps for salaried employees, because the additional employer contribution increases the overall cap for the employees.[1] Some countries actually allow higher contributions from the self-employed into certain types of plans, as is the case in Belgium, France, Japan, and Switzerland (OECD, 2019[2]).

As such, the allowed contributions to the pension schemes should align across different types of workers. Workers who cannot contribute to the BPJS-JP scheme or have lower contribution rates to the BPJS-JHT scheme should still be able to contribute that additional amount to the BPJS-JHT scheme, even if those contributions would not be mandatory.

### 2.1.2. Harmonise the mandatory pension schemes for public and private sector workers

Most OECD countries have taken steps to harmonise the pension schemes for public and private sector workers. The majority have plans that are fully integrated, with no differentiation between the plans of public or private sector workers. A few countries do have a separate scheme for public sector workers, but which offers very similar benefits as for private sector workers. Ten countries provide an additional top-up for public sector workers in addition to the plans that also cover private sector workers. Only four OECD countries have schemes for public sector workers that are entirely separate from those for private sector workers (Belgium, France, Germany, and Korea). Indeed, since the 1990s, 11 OECD countries have reformed the civil service pension schemes to be more aligned with the schemes covering the general population (OECD, 2016[3]).[2]

Indonesia should move towards aligning the mandatory pension schemes for public and private sector workers. The design of the schemes is already similar, with a base DB plan and a DC component as a top-up. However, the benefit accrual and contribution levels differ. Better alignment and integration can present numerous benefits, such as improved equity, transparency, labour mobility, portability, and administrative costs (OECD, 2016[3]).

### 2.1.3. Reformulate the cap on benefits from the BPJS-JP scheme

The cap on benefits from the BPJS-JP scheme could result in declining replacement rates from the scheme over time that could eventually result in a disconnect between the contributions that workers make and the benefits they receive. If the cap on benefits declines significantly compared to wage growth, workers may have to continue contributing to the scheme without gaining any additional entitlement for their pension. This could harm the population's trust and confidence in the system, and lead to increased incentives for workers to become informal or leave the labour market earlier than they would have otherwise planned to do.

The experience in Finland provides an example of how the imposition of a maximum benefit can lead to perverse incentives regarding labour market participation at older ages. Before the 2005 reform abolished the cap, earnings-related pension benefits in Finland were capped at 60% of an individual's highest wage in their career, meaning that many did not benefit from continuing to work at older ages after having reached their maximum benefit. This contributed to a very early effective retirement age of around 57.5 leading up to the reform. Figure 2.1 shows that the removal of the cap, along with other measures to encourage longer working lives such as limiting the ability of people to take an unemployment or disability pension as a pathway to retirement, led to a significant increase in the effective retirement age in the years following the reform (Börsch-Supan, 2005[4]).

**Figure 2.1. Effective retirement age in the earnings-related pension scheme in Finland**

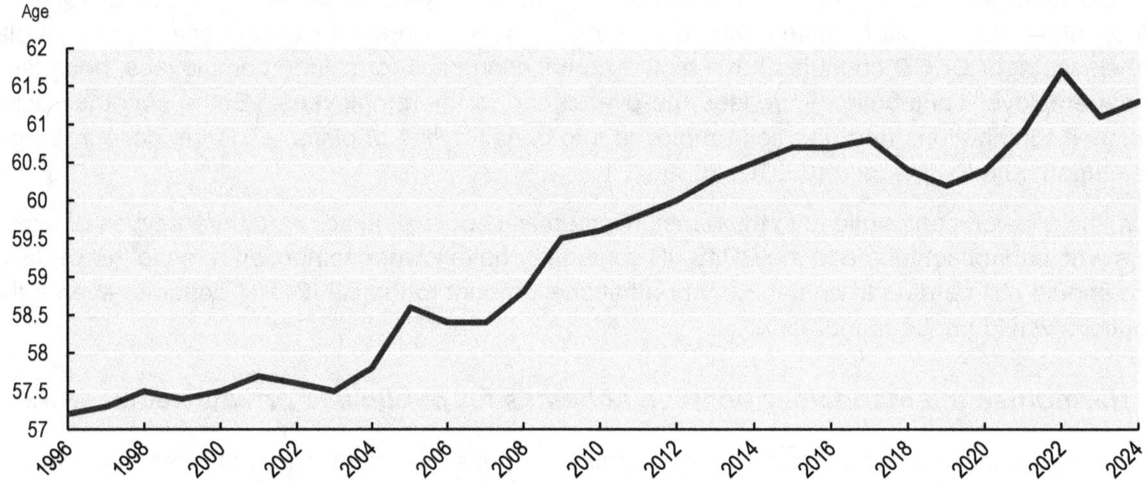


Source: Finnish Center for Pensions (2024[5]), Effective Retirement Age, https://tilastot.etk.fi/pxweb/en/ETK/ETK__130elakkeellesiirtymisika/esiirtymisika01.px/chart/chartViewLine/.

Rather than formulating the benefit cap as an absolute value in total, the cap could instead reflect a maximum value of annual accrual of benefits. This would mean that contributors would accrue benefits at a rate of 1% of salary per year, with a cap on the salary. This formulation would allow all contributors to continue accruing benefits with each additional contribution, while maintaining the redistributive features of the scheme.

### *2.1.4. Align the retirement ages for publicly-provided pension schemes*

The BPJS-JP and BPJS-JHT should align their retirement ages to avoid the incentives to retire earlier and withdraw all assets from the JHT scheme. The average normal retirement age across the OECD in 2020 was 64.4, which increases to 66.3 when accounting for future planned increases (Figure 2.2). The only OECD country having a normal retirement age less than age 60 today is Türkiye, which plans to increase the age from 52 to 65 for new entrants to the labour market.

**Figure 2.2. Current and future normal retirement ages for a man with a full career from age 22**

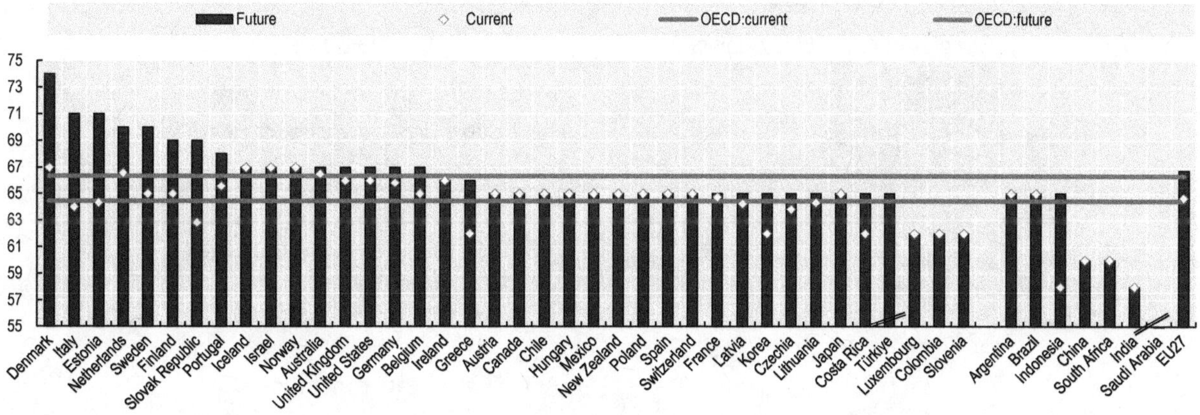


Source: OECD (2023[6]), Pensions at a Glance 2023: OECD and G20 Indicators, https://www.oecd.org/en/publications/pensions-at-a-glance-2023_678055dd-en.html.

### *2.1.5. Align the payout options available for the BPJS-JHT scheme with the objective to finance retirement*

The OECD Recommendation for the Good Design of Defined Contribution Pension Plans states that the design of DC pension plans should be coherent with their long-term purpose and role in the pension system, and that pension systems should ensure protection against longevity risk in retirement (OECD, 2022[7]). The legal mandate of the BPJS is to administer basic pension benefits for the Indonesian population. The BPJS-JHT scheme is mandatory for many workers, and the only contributory pension scheme that most workers have access to. As such, it is likely that savings in the plan with be primarily used to finance an individual's essential spending in retirement. Payouts with guaranteed lifetime income are best suited for meeting essential spending needs because they ensure that the individual will have a certain level of income for life, as illustrated in Figure 2.3. Nevertheless, restrictions around payout options also need allow for some flexibility for circumstances where this option may not be the most suitable, such as when the individual is in poor health or if they have not saved enough to obtain a meaningful level of lifetime income (OECD, 2024[8]).

**Figure 2.3. Illustration of the risks that should be mitigated for different spending needs in retirement and the corresponding type of solution**

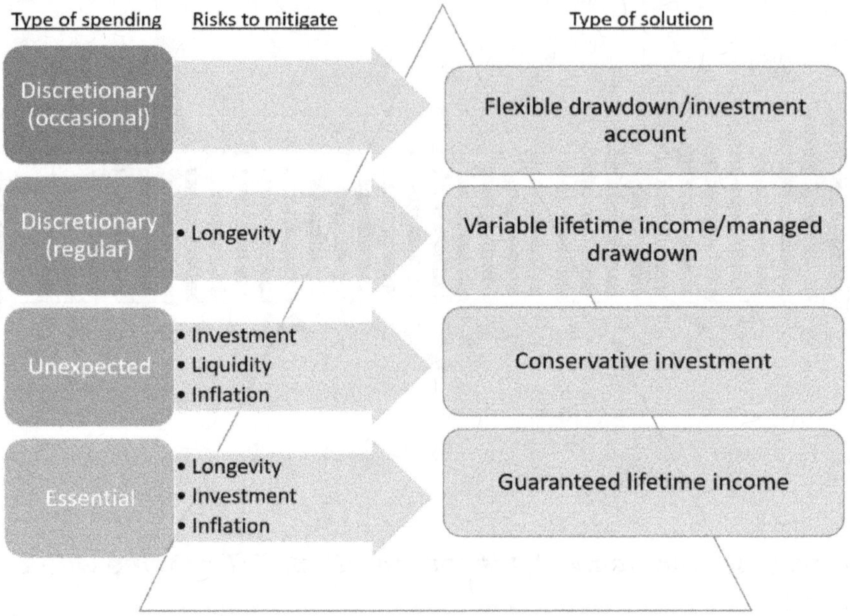


Source: OECD (2024[8]), OECD Pensions Outlook 2024: Improving Asset-backed Pensions for Better Retirement Outcomes and More Resilient Pension Systems, https://www.oecd.org/en/publications/oecd-pensions-outlook-2024_51510909-en.html.

Nevertheless, coherence in design also involves coherence between the design of the accumulation and payout phases. Limiting the options that individuals have to use their savings can also have a detrimental effect on participation in the plan when doing so is voluntary. As such, the main payout option from the BPJS-JHT scheme for those with mandatory participation should be a lifetime income, allowing for exceptions for those with low balances or in poor health. However, additional flexibility could be allowed for those participating in the scheme on a voluntary basis.

### *2.1.6. Make taxation neutral between lump sums and annuities*

The tax treatment of payout options should accommodate, not disincentivise, options providing a regular income. In Indonesia lump sums are taxed favourably in comparison to options providing an income. The objective of the pension system is to encourage individuals to save enough for their retirement. Those who manage to save enough to be able to opt for an annuity should not then be at a relative financial disadvantage because they take a regular income in retirement.

## 2.2. Promote availability of options to accumulate retirement savings and provide retirement income

The pension system in Indonesia faces some challenges with respect to the options available for voluntary pension plans in both the accumulation of retirement savings and in their payout. The number of employer-provided occupational pension plans has been dramatically declining, particularly for DB plans, many of which have either been closed completely or converted to a DC plan. One important driver of this trend has been the introduction of mandatory contributions to the publicly managed schemes, which compete with the resources available to employers to finance an occupational pension plan. For the payout of retirement savings from DC plans, there are currently no options available for people to purchase a lifetime income product when they arrive at retirement.

The Indonesian authorities have taken several measures to limit the unfavourable trends relating to the availability of voluntary pension plans. In an effort to promote competition and efficiency, recent legislation has allowed asset managers to manage pension funds in addition to insurance companies and banks. Legislation also allows employers to convert their pension plans from a DB plan to a DC plan, which could mitigate the number of plan closures by reducing the risks borne by the employers. Employer contributions to pension plans are already tax-deductible, reducing the overall cost for them to contribute to the plans. At retirement, pension savers are now also allowed to opt for a fixed term annuity, rather than being required to purchase a lifetime annuity, to ensure that retirees have a sustainable income option available to them at retirement.

Additional policy options to promote the availability of occupational pension plans and lifetime income options include reducing the cost for employers to establish and manage a plan, allowing for alternative designs of lifetime income products, and considering the establishment of a centralised public annuity provider to ensure supply.

### *2.2.1. Take measures to reduce the costs of opening and administering a plan for employers*

While the offer of an occupational pension plan can present numerous benefits for an employer, the cost of providing a plan can deter many employers from establishing one. Pension benefits add to an employee's remuneration, and therefore can be useful to recruit and retain good employees, ultimately reducing an employer's cost to recruit and train new staff. However, the cost and complexity of setting up a plan are common reasons that prevent employers – particularly smaller employers – to set up a plan (OECD, 2022[9]).

Governments can take various measures to reduce the costs to employers of establishing a pension plan. One way is to provide financial support to employers to set up a new pension plan. In the United States, for example, the government provides a tax credit for smaller employers who set up a plan, and in the United Kingdom providers using the publicly-established pension fund NEST do not have to pay any set-up costs. Another way is to establish a centralised clearinghouse to administer the contributions of employers to a third-party pension provider, thereby reducing the administrative costs of running the plan for employers. Such bodies can be set up within a public institution, which is the approach taken for example in Lithuania, New Zealand, and Mexico. In other countries, such as in Chile and Colombia, the pension providers themselves have taken the initiative to set-up a clearinghouse. Australia has set up a clearinghouse specifically available to small employers (OECD, 2022[9]).

### *2.2.2. Allow non-guaranteed lifetime income options*

Non-guaranteed lifetime income options provide longevity protection to retirees while limiting the risk exposure to providers, which could help to promote the availability of lifetime income options for pensioners. These types of products pool the longevity risk of participants and provide regular income payments, but unlike regular lifetime annuities, the level of the income is adjusted up or down depending on the actual investment and longevity experience of the plan. As such, it is the participants of the plan who collectively bear the investment and systemic longevity risks, while still being protected from the idiosyncratic longevity risk of living longer than the average life expectancy. In addition, as payments are not guaranteed, banks and asset managers could offer such products, not only life insurance companies (OECD, 2022[10]).

### 2.2.3. *Consider establishing a public annuity provider*

Public annuity providers provide lifetime income payments for publicly provided pension plans, or to ensure the supply of lifetime income products when the private sector is unwilling to do so at a competitive price. Several countries with asset-backed mandatory or quasi-mandatory pension schemes, such as Denmark, Lithuania and Sweden rely on publicly established institutions to provide the lifetime income payments to members in retirement. Other countries, such as Croatia and Singapore, have public annuity providers that operate alongside private providers to promote competition in the market, thereby ensuring the availability of cost-efficient products.

Public annuity providers should have robust regulatory and risk management frameworks in place to manage risk exposures and ensure that they will have sufficient capital to make the lifetime payments to their members. If such requirements are not in place, the government will effectively act as the backstop of the provider in case of any solvency problems, which would unfairly shift the cost and risk of providing lifetime income products to the taxpayers. Strong governance frameworks should include internal controls to ensure the entity is complying with regulatory requirements and that the risk management framework is effective.

In Indonesia, the BPJS could provide lifetime income payments for members of the JHT scheme, thereby managing a coherent lifetime pension scheme for both the accumulation and decumulation of retirement savings. For voluntary occupational DC plans, the BPJS could provide lifetime annuities, or alternatively a separate and independent institution could be established to carry out this mandate. Regardless, the governance structure in place would need to ensure the independence of decision making and operations to avoid any potential conflicts of interest with government priorities.

## 2.3. Improve the uptake and use of retirement savings schemes

Indonesia faces a huge challenge relating to the coverage of pension schemes, primarily relating to a lack of participation. There is a large percentage of non-compliance even when participation is mandatory, and voluntary participation in the publicly provided JHT scheme is low. In addition, voluntary pension plans cover only a small percentage of the workforce. Nevertheless, there is likely to be some additional capacity to save for average earning workers, though saving more may be more challenging for those with lower incomes.

Policy options to encourage higher rates of participation and uptake of plans include better enforcement of mandatory participation through the tax authority and providing matching contributions to participants.

### 2.3.1. *Enforce mandates through the tax authority*

To combat the low level of compliance with mandatory contributions to pension schemes, Indonesia could rely on the tax authority to enforce those mandates. Several countries have relied on this approach to ensure that workers contribute the required amounts to the funded pension schemes. In Iceland and Israel, the tax authority checks that workers have made their required contributions when individuals submit their income declarations and follows up with the workers who fail to comply. Other countries take specific measures to enforce mandatory contributions for the self-employed, which can be harder to impose. For example, in Chile, tax is withheld each year from the self-employed to fulfil their contribution obligations for the following year.

### 2.3.2. *Provide matching contributions*

Many jurisdictions use government-provided matching contributions to promote retirement savings and to help low-income people in particular to build up retirement savings even though they may have a lower capacity to save. Matching contributions are additional contributions that the government or employer makes for every contribution the individual makes, often calculated as a proportion of the individual's contribution and normally subject to a maximum amount. Matching contributions can also specifically target lower income groups. For example, the Australian government provides a matching contribution for voluntary contributions made by those having an income below a certain threshold. In Chile, the government provides matching contributions for younger employees between the ages of 18 and 25 who make less than 150% of the minimum wage for their first 24 months of contributions, to increase savings for those who are most likely to benefit it. In Colombia, the government provides a matching contribution at the point of retirement rather than at the time of contributing to increase the amount of savings members have available at retirement (OECD, 2024[8]).

## 2.4. Encourage diversified investment strategies that are appropriate for the goal of financing retirement

While some improvements have been made, the existing rules and limits relating to investment tend to lead to investment strategies that are overly conservative and lack diversification. Legislation passed in 2023 addressed one of these problems for the BPJS plans by allowing them to sell their assets at a loss, thereby eliminating the 'cut loss' problem. However, the positive effects of this measure may take some time to materialise as asset managers adjust their investment approach. Authorities also made it mandatory for voluntary defined contribution plans to offer a lifecycle investment strategy. However, lifecycle funds are only mandatory as an option for employee contributions, and all investments are still subject to a minimum investment in government bonds of 30%. Additionally, pension funds are prevented from investing abroad, and local opportunities for long-term investment and other vehicles or instruments appropriate for retirement remain limited.

In addition, plan sponsors and investment managers lack incentives to implement investment strategies that are more appropriate for the goal of financing retirement. The BPJS is not required to report their investment performance, which impedes the measurement and assessment of their investment approach. For voluntary pensions, occupational plans are primarily used to fund employers' severance liabilities, creating an incentive to minimise the risk of loss of capital to ensure they can pay the severance liabilities when they are due rather than to maximise long-term investment returns. The authorities have taken some measures to address this issue. Recent legislation reduced the severance benefits that employees are entitled to, and will require that employers send contributions to fund the liabilities for lower-income employees to the JHT scheme. However, employers will still be able to use occupational pension funds to finance their liability to employees earning over the threshold.

Finally, there is a lack of investment knowledge in the governance and oversight of pension funds which further limits their ability to implement and oversee appropriate strategies. For the BPJS and voluntary plans, not all members of the governing bodies are required to have any technical knowledge of pensions.

Policy options to promote diversified investment strategies that are appropriate for the goal of financing retirement include removing minimum requirements to invest in government bonds, relaxing restrictions around foreign investment, making lifecycle investment funds the default strategies, developing performance benchmarks and metrics, removing the possibility to finance severance benefits through pension funds, and strengthening the investment expertise of the governing bodies.

### *2.4.1. Remove the minimum requirement for voluntary pension plans to invest in government bonds*

The OECD's Core Principles of Private Pension Regulation recommend against having minimum investment limits in place for any given category of investment, and more generally any limit that could impede adequate diversification (OECD, 2016[11]). Having a minimum required investment of 30% in Indonesian government bonds presents significant concentration risk, which could threaten the solvency of pension funds in the case of default. In addition, having a minimum limit in government bonds can prevent investment managers from investing in higher levels of equity, even when such a strategy could be in the best interests of members investing over a long-term horizon for their retirement.

### *2.4.2. Gradually relax restrictions around foreign investment*

The restriction on investing abroad imposes significant limitations on pension funds to implement a well-diversified investment strategy. In the OECD, investments abroad make up a significant portion of pension funds' investment. In 2023, OECD countries had on average 46% of pension assets invested abroad (OECD, 2024[12]).[3] In jurisdictions where restrictions on foreign investment have been relaxed, pension funds have often followed suit by increasing their investments abroad, demonstrating an appetite for international diversification. This is evident in Peru, where the foreign investment by pension funds has increased along with the regular increase in the foreign investment limits since the early 2000s (Figure 2.4). Similarly, in Chile restrictions on foreign investment were gradually relaxed from 2006 to 2013, with foreign investment by pension funds correspondingly increasing from 32% to 42% over that period. South Africa has also gradually increased the allowed foreign investment since 2006, driving the increase in pension fund investment abroad from 4% in 2006 to 20% in 2019. Indirect restrictions on foreign investment can also impede diversified investment. For example, limits on foreign currency exposures and derivative investment in Croatia have presented an obstacle for pension funds to invest abroad. However, following the adoption of the Euro at the beginning of 2023, it became easier for them to invest elsewhere in Europe, and foreign investment by pension funds increased from 21.6% in 2022 to 27.6% in 2023 (OECD, 2024[13]).

**Figure 2.4. Foreign investment limits and actual foreign investment by pension funds in Peru**

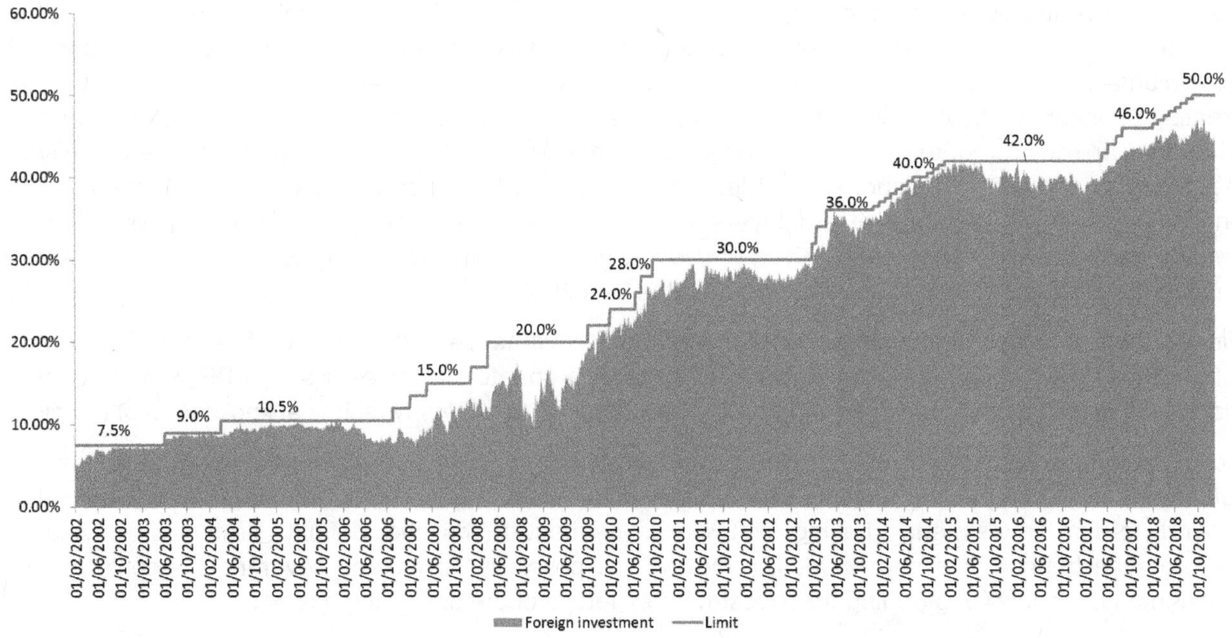


Source: OECD, (2019[14]), OECD Reviews of Pension Systems, https://www.oecd.org/en/publications/oecd-reviews-of-pension-systems-peru_e80b4071-en.html.

### *2.4.3. Expand the use of lifecycle investment strategies for DC plans to increase investment risk exposure at younger ages*

While voluntary pension plans must offer lifecycle investment strategies as an option for employee contributions, this is not the default strategy and employer contributions do not follow this approach.

The OECD Recommendation for the Good Design of Defined Contribution Pension Plans highlights that lifecycle investment strategies that take on more investment risk at younger ages and gradually reduce the risk exposure as individuals approach retirement can be appropriate default strategies for pension fund investment (OECD, 2022[7]). These strategies allow for the possibility for members to earn higher returns early in their working life when they still have the time to recover from negative shocks to the market, while mitigating the risk that they will experience large shocks just before retirement that could be significantly detrimental to the amount of retirement income they would be able to finance.

Conservative investment strategies can be extremely detrimental to retirement savers, as they will lose out on the potential upside of investing in higher growth assets over the long term. Reforms to the default investment strategy in the Slovak Republic illustrate the magnitude of such choices. In 2013, the government transferred around 90% of pension savers to pension funds investing in fixed income. As a result, the level of investment earnings savers missed out on is estimated to be between 2 and 8 billion euros (Ódor and Povala, 2020[15]). Savers investing in an equity index would have accumulated more than twice the amount of assets by 2023, and even those investing in a slightly higher level of risk of a mixed equity and bond fund would have accumulated over 20% more.

OECD calculations illustrate the benefits of investing in more diversified investment strategies, including lifecycle strategies, compared to solely investing in domestic fixed income. The coloured bars in Figure 2.5 show the total additional accumulated asset with a diversified equity portfolio, a diversified 60/40 portfolio in bonds/equities, a life-cycle investment strategy reducing the equity exposure 10 years before retirement, and the life-cycle investment strategy reducing the equity exposure 20 years before retirement, compared to a domestic fixed income portfolio. In all cases, the vast majority of cohorts across all countries shown would have been significantly better off investing in a strategy other than domestic fixed income (OECD, 2024[8]).

**Figure 2.5. Average difference in accumulated assets when the equity portfolios are superior to the portfolio with fixed income and vice-versa, by country**

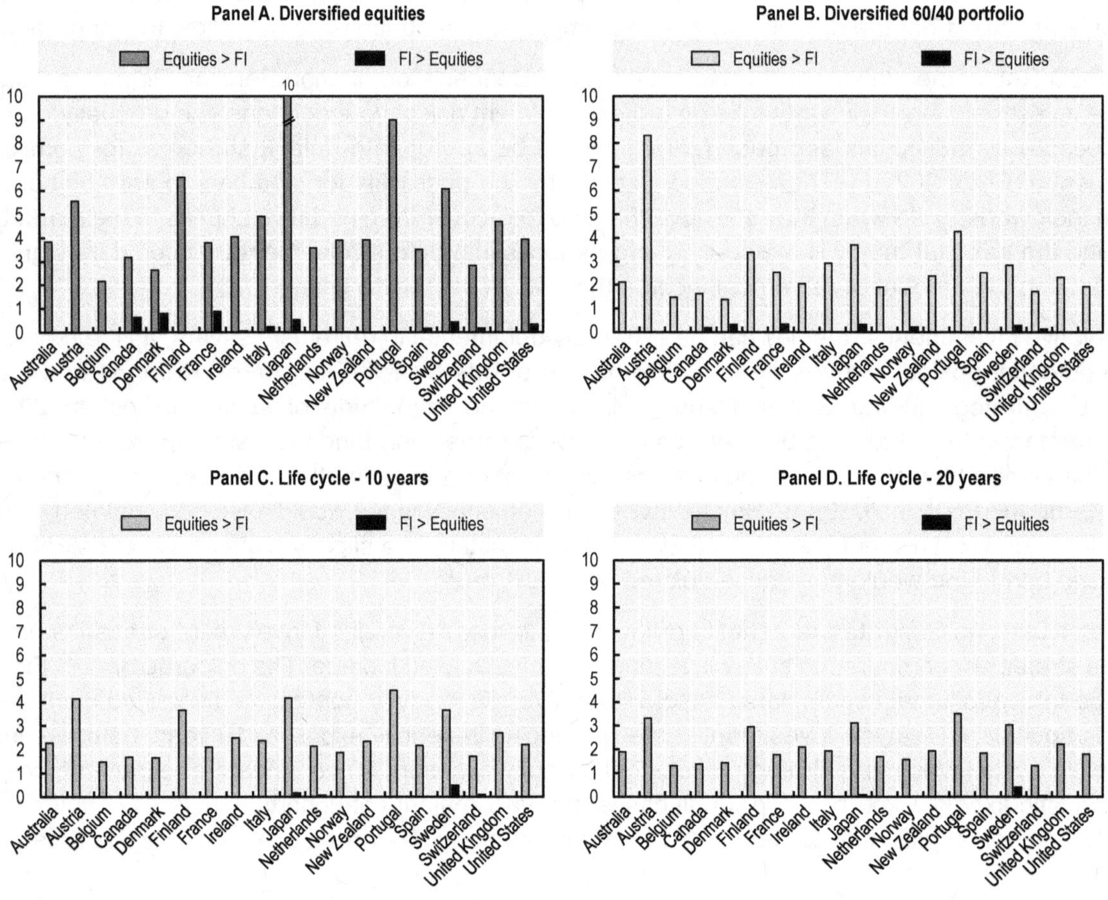


Note: FI means fixed income.

Source: OECD (2024[8]), OECD Pensions Outlook 2024: Improving Asset-backed Pensions for Better Retirement Outcomes and More Resilient Pension Systems, https://www.oecd.org/en/publications/oecd-pensions-outlook-2024_51510909-en.html.

Lifecycle investment strategies could be the default investment strategy for individuals contributing to voluntary pension plans. They could also potentially be implemented for participants in the BPJS-JHT.

### *2.4.4. Develop performance benchmarks and metrics appropriate for a long-term investment horizon*

Performance measurement and assessment should improve across the entire pension system in Indonesia to better align the metrics and benchmarks with the investment horizon and objective of the pension funds. The BPJS does not currently report accurate investment return calculations by which performance can be assessed. Voluntary pension funds report annualised investment returns, however benchmarks to compare the investment performance of funds do not seem to be used.

The measurement and assessment of the investment performance of pension funds needs to be consistent with their long-term investment horizon and objective to finance retirement. The OECD Core Principles of Private Pension Regulation further specify that that performance benchmarks need to reflect the risk level of the strategy and be clear and objective (OECD, 2016[11]).

Ideally, the measure of investment performance of pension funds should consider a period longer than one year to dampen the volatility and provide a more accurate picture of long-term returns. When reporting and comparing the investment returns of pension plans, the OECD's Pension Markets In Focus reports not only the returns over the last year, but also the average returns over the last 5, 10, 15, and 20 years where data is available (OECD, 2023[16]).

Performance benchmarks used to assess the investment performance of pension funds should also be reflective of the asset allocation and strategy chosen. Such benchmarks can be constructed based on a weighted average of benchmark returns for different asset classes, typically referencing passive indices. Performance can also be compared to the benchmark for different time horizons to help identify whether the selected investment strategy is underperforming compared to the market average. In Australia, for example, the regulator has developed a heatmap that assesses the investment performance of pension funds over three-, five- and eight-year horizons using multiple benchmarking methods in order to provide different perspectives regarding their investment performance. One benchmark is a simple reference portfolio of passive, low-cost and liquid investments in order to assess the added value of the investment strategy selected by the pension funds. Another benchmark reflects the fund's strategic asset allocation to assess their implementation of the investment strategy (APRA, 2022[17]).

### *2.4.5. Eliminate the possibility to finance severance benefits with occupational pension funds*

The use of occupational pension funds to finance the severance liabilities of employers presents a conflict of interest with the objective that pension funds should have to finance the retirement benefits of employees. Rather than striving to achieve long-term investment returns in line with the objective to finance retirement, the objective of the fund becomes to preserve capital to be paid out when an employee leaves the organisation. This has resulted in investment portfolios weighted towards cash and deposits.

The severance benefit programme is distinct from the voluntary occupational pension programme, and the two programmes should not be combined into the same financing vehicle. Any pre-funded severance liability programme should be established as a fund separate from the occupational pension plan.

### *2.4.6. Increase requirements around investment expertise in the governance framework*

The governing bodies of pension funds do not necessarily have the investment expertise needed to inform strategic investment decisions or supervise the implementation of the investment policy. The only member of the governing body of the BPJS required to have pensions expertise is the independent expert. For voluntary pension funds, only the management board is required to have technical knowledge, while there are no requirements for the supervisory board to have technical knowledge of pensions or investment.

There are three main approaches to increase the investment expertise in the governance framework. The first is to increase the knowledge requirements for the members of the governing body. The second is to impose educational requirements for the members of the governing body to provide them the opportunity to increase and maintain their knowledge. The third is to establish expert committees to advise the governing body on the decisions they need to make.

Governing body members are often held to minimum standards with respect to qualifications or expertise. Such requirements can refer generally to professional or management experience or require more specific knowledge of certain topics such as investment. Occasionally, as is the case in Australia and Estonia, regulators require that the governing body members formally demonstrate their technical capabilities before being allowed to become a member of a board.

Another option is to impose educational requirements on board members to ensure that they have the opportunity to acquire any knowledge they may be lacking. Ireland, for example, requires that trustees receive training within the first six months of their appointment, and continue to receive regular training at least every two years after that. In the Netherlands, members of governing bodies are required to take regular courses on the investment and governance of pensions to make sure they maintain the relevant knowledge. Several jurisdictions are also making efforts to increase the accessibility of training. For example, the regulator in the United Kingdom offers e-learning courses for trustees to follow online.

Another approach to address a lack of expertise is to establish expert committees to advise the governing body. Investment is a common focus of such committees. The committees are normally made up of at least one member of the governing body along with the experts, and are occasionally mandated, as is the case in Israel. Such committees could be particularly useful to establish for the Board of the BPJS. The supervisory board of voluntary pension funds can already have advisory committees on certain topics, one of which is risk monitoring. This committee could include a focus on investment risk, and the requirement to establish such a committee could be expanded to smaller funds.

## 2.5. Strengthen the sustainability of defined benefit pension funds

Measures should be taken to ensure the sustainability of both the BPJS-JP DB scheme and the DPPK DB schemes in the long term. Contributions to the BPJS-JP scheme are not adequate to provide the promised benefits in the long-term. DPPK DB pension schemes are allowed too much flexibility in how they value their liabilities and funding levels, which impedes a proper assessment of their solvency risk and puts members at an increased risk of losing their benefits.

Several measures could be considered to strengthen the sustainability of defined benefit pension funds. The parameters of these plans need to adapt to ensure that the contributions made to the schemes are sufficient to finance the promised benefits. To further protect members from the risk of insolvency of voluntary occupational DB plans, authorities could consider introducing a pension guarantee fund, though this would need to account for the potential downsides of doing so.

### *2.5.1. Increase contributions to the BPJS-JP DB scheme to ensure sustainability*

Contributions to the BPJS-JP scheme are currently 3% of salary, which is largely insufficient to finance the annual accrued benefit of 1% of salary. Without increases in the contributions or downward adjustments to benefits, the scheme will rapidly become a PAYG scheme with benefits financed by the contributions of current workers rather than by the invested contributions made by the members over their lifetime. While Indonesia is currently a relatively young country with an old-age dependency ratio of around 10%, this ratio has been following a regular upward trend since the 1950s.[4] This ratio can only be expected to increase further with decreasing fertility and increasing life expectancy. Fertility rates in Indonesia are currently around replacement, with 2.17 births per women in 2021, down from over 5 births per women in the 1960s (Roser, 2024[18]). As with other countries experiencing rapidly increasing old-age dependency ratios, PAYG pension schemes eventually will come under financing pressure, particularly if contributions are not representative of the cost of financing benefits, and future generations of workers will unfairly be forced to bear the consequences. Indeed, the productive share of the population is projected to decline after 2030 (OECD, 2024[19]). The BPJS-JP scheme is still young, and Indonesia still has the opportunity to ensure its long-term financial sustainability by setting contributions at a level that is actuarially fair, which will also promote intergenerational equity for the participants of the plan.

### *2.5.2. Strengthen requirements around the assumptions used to value liabilities and calculate funding for voluntary occupational DB plans*

The valuation of liabilities and calculation of funding positions of defined benefit plans need to reflect the actual financial obligations that the plans will have to pay to their members to ensure sufficient contributions to the plan and protect their long-term solvency. Currently, there are no requirements around the discount rate and mortality rate assumptions used to value pension liabilities. Actuaries can set the discount rates used to value DPPK DB plans at a level above the expected investment return on assets, implying that the calculated funding ratios would then overestimate the funding position of the plans. In addition, funding ratios can reflect the contributions receivable that have not been paid into the plan, adding to the uncertainty that assets will be sufficient to finance future liabilities. Plans are given the flexibility to choose their preferred valuation methodology, increasing the lack of comparability of funding positions across plans.

Regulatory requirements should establish the basic requirements for the assumptions and methodology used for the valuation of pension liabilities to ensure their adequacy and a certain level of comparability across schemes. It is common for there to be legislative requirements around such calculations (Ellis, Kivisaari and Stańko, 2015[20]). Requirements usually establish a minimum standard for the assumptions and calculations related to plan funding.

The assumptions and methodology appropriate to calculate liabilities and funding ratios should link to the objective of the calculation. If the objective is to assess the current level of funding of the plan, valuation using the risk-free rate under the solvency termination methodology is the most transparent and comparable assumption to use, and allows a clear picture of whether the current assets are sufficient to finance the future expected benefit obligations (OECD, 2020[21]). Nevertheless, valuation based on a going concern perspective using a discount rate based on the expected return of assets may be more useful for strategic decision making relating to issues such as the investment strategy and the contribution rates. Having multiple calculations provides a more complete perspective of the funding situation of the plan. Canada, for example, requires DB pension funds to assess their funding levels using different methodologies to have different views on the funding status of each plan (OECD, 2020[21]).

There should be a requirement for the mortality assumptions to reflect realistic expectations. The current level of mortality should be reflective of the mortality experience of the plan members, and assumptions should account for future expected improvement. Jurisdictions take varied approaches to establishing the requirements around mortality assumptions. Some jurisdictions, such as Chile, require providers to use the mortality tables prescribed by the regulators. Others, such as Denmark, require that providers justify any deviation of assumptions from the table developed by the supervisor. Canada requires that providers use the tables developed by the actuarial association, while in the United Kingdom those tables are recommended but not required (Mosher, 2023[22]). Regardless, pension funds should be able to demonstrate the appropriateness of the mortality assumptions to justify the appropriateness of their use.

### *2.5.3. Prioritise ensuring adequate funding levels of occupational DB plans before considering the introduction of a pension protection fund*

Members of voluntary occupational DB plans have little protection in the case of insolvency of the plan sponsor. The risk of default is increased by the lack of investment diversification and the overstatement of funding ratios. One option the Indonesian authorities have discussed to increase the protection of members' benefits from DB plans would be to introduce a pension protection fund. Nevertheless, such a measure could lead to negative unintended consequences.

Pension protection funds guarantee the payment of at least a portion of the pension benefits promised by DB plans. These funds effectively act as an insurance for plan members against the insolvency of the plan sponsor. The funds can either take over the management and responsibility of the plan, insure the plan via the purchase of an external annuity, or inject funds to make up any deficit. The first two options are the interventions that protection funds most commonly rely upon.

Normally, plan sponsors must pay a premium to the fund for the insurance offered. Insurance premiums should reflect the underlying probability that the insurance will be triggered, which is driven by the underlying risks. There are three key risks that drive the probability that the protection fund will be triggered. The first is sponsor strength. If the sponsor is in a weak financial position, they are more likely to face insolvency. The second is the underfunding of the plan. The larger the plan deficit, the more likely the sponsor will default on its obligations to the plan. The third is the investment strategy taken. The riskier the investment strategy, the more likely it is that the plan will face large losses that it may not be able to recover from in time to meet its payment obligations. Nevertheless, premiums do not often fully reflect the underlying risk that the fund will be triggered, which creates a disconnect between the finances available to the protection fund and its potential liability, increasing the risk that it will not be able to fulfil its role as a guarantor of benefits.

Table 2.1 summarises some examples of pension protection funds that exist in the OECD. It includes the intervention they take in the case that the fund is triggered, as well as the basis for the premium. Most premiums are higher for underfunded plans, but only one fund also accounts for sponsor strength and no fund also accounts for the investment strategy the plan employs.

### Table 2.1. Pension protection funds intervention procedure and premium basis

| Country | Intervention | Premium basis | | |
|---|---|---|---|---|
| | | Sponsor strength | Underfunding | Investment strategy |
| Canada | Payment | No | Yes | No |
| Germany | Annuities | No | No | No |
| Japan | Takeover | No | Yes | No |
| Sweden | Annuities | No | Yes | No |
| Switzerland | Annuities | No | Yes | No |
| United Kingdom | Takeover | Yes | Yes | No |
| United States | Takeover | No | Yes | No |

Source: Broeders and Chen (2013[23]), Pension Benefit Security: A Comparison of Solvency Requirements, a Pension Guarantee Fund, and Sponsor Support https://www.jstor.org/stable/24548150.

The challenge with enforcing risk-based premiums for protection funds is that sponsors having a higher risk of defaulting on their pension obligations are also the least likely to be able to afford higher premiums. Requiring higher premiums could in turn increase their risk of default, which could also present higher systemic risk for the protection fund as sponsor defaults tend to be pro-cyclical, being more likely in difficult markets. In addition, risk-based premiums would increase the cost of the protection fund for most firms, rendering it unaffordable and acting as a disincentive from offering a pension plan at all.

Given the current trend to close voluntary DB occupational plans, the introduction of a pension protection fund requiring additional premiums from sponsors would likely accelerate these trends. As such, the introduction of risk-based premiums would therefore be even more difficult, and the government would likely have to act as the backstop of such fund if it was unable to cover the defaulted obligations of sponsors.

Therefore, the initial focus to improve the protection of benefits of members of occupational DB plans should be to shore up the funding of these plans. Once the market is more stable, authorities could consider whether the introduction of a protection fund would be feasible and beneficial overall.

## 2.6. Align schemes' design with clear objectives that aim to ensure complementarity of the different components of the system

A key priority of the government is to further harmonise the pension system to ensure the complementarity of the different components. The institutional framework for the management of social benefits has been streamlined into two institutions managing employment and health-related benefits. Other measures have aimed to improve the efficiency of voluntary pension plans and facilitating members' transition to retirement. Retirement ages are now also standardised across voluntary pension funds to promote the use of benefits from the plans to finance retirement. Nevertheless, there is no clear objective regarding the severance pay system, which is not benefiting those that it should. The BPJS-JHT fails in its objective to improve financial security in retirement because assets are largely withdrawn well before retirement. A new measure to increase mandatory savings for higher-income workers aims to improve replacement rates in retirement, but will concern only a minority of workers and is not targeted at those who are at higher risk of inadequate benefits.

Policy measures should ensure that each component of the system has a clear objective that it aims to fulfil within the overall objective of the pension system, and that the design of each component is conducive to achieving that goal.

### *2.6.1. Replace the severance pay system with increased employer contributions to the BPJS-JHT*

The severance pay system lacks a clear objective, and it is not designed in a way that actually benefits those it intends to help. While the programme pays benefits at retirement, it is not designed to complement the other pension programmes in a targeted manner. Even though it is mandatory, employer compliance is low and only employees of the largest companies actually benefit. Additionally, the benefits paid only reflect the length of employment at the last employer, and not the employee's full career. Those who receive benefits are therefore often not those who are most in need of them, and there is little relationship between the benefits that the individual will receive in their retirement and their employment over their lifetime.

Retirement benefits linked to employment should reflect the entire career of the individual. The proposal of the authorities to require funding of severance liabilities in the JHT scheme could improve this link, so long as the contributions are made to an account that the individual is able to keep when they change jobs. However, this design lacks any distinction from requiring employer contributions to the BPJS-JHT scheme and eliminating the severance plans.

An alternative would simply be to replace the severance programme with increased employer contributions to the BPJS-JHT scheme. In addition to retirement benefits, as currently designed the JHT also pays benefits if the member dies or has a disability, so the provision of these benefits from the severance scheme could also be replaced by the JHT scheme.

### *2.6.2. Forbid early withdrawals form the BPJS-JHT scheme except for exceptional individual circumstances*

The OECD Recommendation for the Good Design of Defined Contribution Pension Plans recommends that "any early access to retirement savings should be a measure of last resort and based on individuals' specific hardship circumstances" (OECD, 2022[7]). Currently, savings in the BPJS-JHT scheme are very easy to withdraw, as savers can withdraw all their savings when they change jobs if they have contributed at least five years. The government tried to introduce a law limiting withdrawals to 10% of savings contingent on having contributed at least ten years, but following protests the law was never passed.

The ability for individuals to fully withdraw their savings from the JHT scheme undermines its purpose to complement the BPJS-JP scheme in improving the adequacy of financing for retirement. Rather than serving to improve financial outcomes in retirement, it is being used for everyday purposes when changing jobs. In recognition of these two distinct uses and objectives, the government is considering splitting the JHT accounts into one that can be used in case of exceptional needs, such as unemployment or health issues, and one that must be reserved for retirement.

The limited use of retirement savings to aid individuals in exceptional individual circumstances is in line with the OECD Recommendation, and it may not be necessary to add complexity by splitting the account into two as long as the conditions to withdraw from the account remain limited to individual circumstances that may lead to hardship. Additionally, limiting the amount that can be withdrawn rather than allowing withdrawals of the whole account could ensure that at least a portion of the savings will go towards its intended purpose. Limiting early withdrawals from the JHT would also remove this impediment for the pension funds to implement investment strategies more focused on the long term.

### *2.6.3. Clarify the objective of the new mandatory pension programme and ensure the alignment of its design with that objective*

Law 4/2023 introduced a new mandatory pension programme for those earning more than IDR 10 million as part of the government's efforts to meet its overarching objective to achieve replacement rates of 40% by 2033. Nevertheless, this programme will only impact the retirement savings of around 5% of the working population.

The objective of this additional programme is not clear, particularly as it is more likely to impact the population that would already have access to an occupational pension plan, or in other words those who are better off and working in medium to large size companies. These groups already have the highest expected replacement rates, so they are less likely to be at risk of having insufficient financial resources in retirement.

Having additional mandatory pension contributions for higher earners, particularly when those contributions are intended to finance individual retirement savings and not part of a scheme involving some redistribution across income levels, can be useful if they have lower replacement rates. One example of a country who takes this approach with asset-backed pensions is in Sweden, where high earners are required to make higher contributions to the quasi-mandatory occupational pension plans. However, the public pension benefits in Sweden are rather progressive, meaning that low-income workers receive higher replacement rates. The rationale for higher contributions for high earners to the occupational pension plans is therefore to avoid that high-income earners have much lower replacement rates than low-income earners.

The objective to equalise replacement rates across income groups is not a clearly stated objective of this new pension programme, although the benefits from the mandatory schemes in Indonesia are also somewhat progressive due to the benefit cap imposed. However, many low-income workers are excluded from the BPJS-JP scheme, so additional contributions for the highest earners could be expected to exacerbate financial inequalities in retirement.

Another consideration for implementing a mandatory pension programme based on a salary threshold are the incentives for employers or employees to be above or below that threshold. For example, employees earning around the threshold may prefer to negotiate a lower salary for other additional benefits to avoid the extra contribution. If employers are expected to contribute, they may try to avoid offering salaries above the threshold, reducing overall pay to employees.

## Policy options for addressing the challenges in the Indonesian asset-backed pension system

**Ensure that the rules of the pension system allow individuals to accumulate adequate retirement savings**

- ***Align contribution limits across different types of workers***. Employees of small and micro enterprises and informal workers have lower contribution ceilings for the publicly managed pension schemes than employees of medium and large enterprises.
- ***Harmonise the mandatory pension schemes for public and private sector workers***. While the design of the schemes is similar, with a base defined benefit plan and an additional defined contribution component, the benefit accrual and contribution levels differ and public sector workers benefit from higher expected replacement rates.
- ***Reformulate the cap on benefits from the BPJS-JP scheme***. The current cap may result in declining replacement rates from the scheme over time which could eventually result in workers having to continue contributing to the scheme without accruing additional benefits.
- ***Align the retirement ages for publicly provided pension schemes***. The retirement age for the mandatory defined contribution plan for private sector workers is 56 while the retirement age for the mandatory defined benefit plan is gradually increasing to 65. Most workers therefore retire at age 56.
- ***Align the payout options from the mandatory defined contribution schemes with the objective to finance retirement***. Savings can currently only be taken as a lump sum and not as an income in retirement.
- ***Make taxation neutral between lump sums and annuities***. Lump sums are currently taxed more favourably than options providing an income.

**Promote availability of options to accumulate retirement savings and provide retirement income available**

- ***Take additional measures to reduce the costs of opening and administering a plan to encourage employers to offer them***. There is currently a trend to close occupational pension plans despite existing measures to improve their attractiveness to employers.
- ***Allow non-guaranteed lifetime income options for payout***. This could help to overcome the lack of availability of lifetime income solutions by reducing the risk exposure to providers.
- ***Consider a public annuity provider***. This can be a solution to ensure the supply of lifetime income products where private provision is lacking.

**Improve the uptake and use of retirement savings schemes needs**

- ***The tax authority could play a role in enforcing compliance with contributing to mandatory schemes***. Currently only 38% of formal workers participate in a mandatory retirement savings scheme.
- ***Promote matching contributions to encourage participation***. These can help low-income people in particular to build up retirement savings even though they may have a lower capacity to save.

**Encourage diversified investment strategies that are appropriate for the goal of financing retirement**

- ***Remove the minimum requirement for voluntary pension plans to invest in government bonds***. The plans must currently invest at least 30% of their assets in Indonesian government bonds.
- ***Gradually relax restrictions around foreign investment***. Pension funds are not currently able to invest abroad, limiting their investment opportunities.
- ***Expand the use of default lifecycle investment strategies for defined contribution plans to increase investment risk exposure at younger ages***. While pension funds must offer these strategies as an option for contributions from employees, this is not the default option and they are not in use for employer or mandatory contributions.
- ***Develop performance benchmarks and metrics appropriate for a long-term investment horizon***. The BPJS does not currently report accurate investment return calculations by which performance can be assessed, and voluntary pension funds lack benchmarks to assess their investment performance.
- ***Eliminate the possibility to finance severance benefits through occupational pension funds***. The use of occupational funds to finance the severance liabilities of employers presents a conflict of interest with the objective that pension funds should have to finance the retirement benefits of employees.
- ***Strengthen requirements around investment expertise in the governance framework*** The governing bodies of pension funds do not necessarily have the investment expertise needed to inform strategic investment decisions or supervise the implementation of the investment policy.

**Strengthen the sustainability of defined benefit pension funds**

- ***Increase contributions to the BPJS-JP scheme to ensure sustainability***. Without increases in the contributions or downward adjustments to benefits, the scheme will rapidly become a PAYG scheme with benefits financed by the contributions of current workers rather than by the invested contributions made by the members over their lifetime.
- ***Strengthen requirements around the assumptions used to value liabilities and calculate funding for voluntary occupational defined benefit plans***. Currently, there are no requirements around the discount rate and mortality rate assumptions used to value pension liabilities.
- ***Prioritise ensuring adequate funding levels of occupational defined benefit plans before considering the introduction of a pension protection fund.*** The introduction of a protection fund to guarantee occupational pension promises in the case of sponsor default would require additional premiums from sponsors and would likely accelerate trends to close occupational plans. The initial focus to improve the protection of benefits of members of occupational defined benefit plans should therefore be to shore up their funding.

**Align schemes' design with clear objectives that aim to ensure complementarity of the different components of the system**

- ***Increase employer contributions to the mandatory defined contribution scheme for private sector workers to replace the severance pay system***. The severance pay system lacks a clear objective, and it is not designed in a way that actually benefits those it intends to help.

- ***Allow early withdrawals from the mandatory defined contribution scheme for private sector workers only for exceptional individual circumstances***. The ability for individuals to fully withdraw their savings from the scheme is not in line with the objective to finance retirement and undermines its purpose to complement the defined benefit scheme in improving the adequacy retirement benefits.
- ***Clarify the objective of the new mandatory pension programme that increases contributions for higher-income employees to ensure the alignment of its design with that objective.*** The programme is more likely to impact the population that would have access to an occupational pension plan and that already have higher expected replacement rates for retirement.

## References

APRA (2022), *Methodology Paper: My Super Heatmap*, https://www.apra.gov.au/sites/default/files/2022-12/Methodology%20paper%20-%20MySuper%20Heatmap.pdf. [17]

Börsch-Supan, A. (2005), *The 2005 Pension Reform in Finland*, https://www.julkari.fi/bitstream/handle/10024/129075/The2005pensionreforminFinland.pdf?sequence=1&isAllowed=y. [4]

Broeders, D. and A. Chen (2013), "Pension Benefit Security: A Comparison of Solvency Requirements, a Pension Guarantee Fund, and Sponsor Support", *The Journal of Risk and Insurance*, Vol. 80/2, pp. 239-272, https://www.jstor.org/stable/24548150. [23]

Ellis, S., E. Kivisaari and D. Stańko (2015), *Synthesis Paper: The role of actuarial calculations and reviews in pension supervision*, https://www.iopsweb.org/WP_23_Synthesis-paper-actuarial%20calculations.pdf. [20]

Finnish Center for Pensions (2024), *Effective Retirement Age*, https://tilastot.etk.fi/pxweb/en/ETK/ETK__130elakkeellesiirtymisika/esiirtymisika01.px/chart/chartViewLine/ (accessed on  May 2025). [5]

Mosher, J. (2023), "Global approaches to developing standard mortality tables for the provision of retirement income", in *Mortality and the Provision of Retirement Income*, OECD Publishing, Paris, https://doi.org/10.1787/4e3f2fb6-en. [22]

Ódor, Ľ. and P. Povala (2020), *Sporiteľ na prvom mieste. Ako zreformovať druhý dôchodkový pilier na Slovensku?*, https://www.nbs.sk/_img/documents/publik/op_1_2020_odor_povala_ako_zreformovat_druhy_pilier.pdf. [15]

OECD (2024), *OECD Data Explorer*, https://data-explorer.oecd.org/vis?lc=en&df[ds]=dsDisseminateFinalDMZ&df[id]=DSD_FP%40DF_WI&df[ag]=OECD.DAF.CM&df[vs]=1.0&dq=.A..PT_AS._T._T._T&lom=LASTNPERIODS&lo=5&to[TIME_PERIOD]=false. [13]

OECD (2024), *OECD Economic Surveys: Indonesia 2024*, OECD Publishing, Paris, https://doi.org/10.1787/de87555a-en. [19]

OECD (2024), *OECD Pensions Outlook 2024: Improving Asset-backed Pensions for Better Retirement Outcomes and More Resilient Pension Systems*, OECD Publishing, Paris, https://doi.org/10.1787/51510909-en. [8]

OECD (2024), *Pension Markets in Focus 2024*, OECD Publishing, Paris, https://doi.org/10.1787/b11473d3-en. [12]

OECD (2023), *Pension Markets in Focus 2023*, OECD Publishing, Paris, https://doi.org/10.1787/28970baf-en. [16]

OECD (2023), *Pensions at a Glance 2023: OECD and G20 Indicators*, OECD Publishing, Paris, https://doi.org/10.1787/678055dd-en. [6]

OECD (2022), "How best to involve employers in the provision of asset-backed pension arrangements", in *OECD Pensions Outlook 2022*, OECD Publishing, Paris, https://doi.org/10.1787/41f6fe2a-en. [9]

OECD (2022), "Policy lessons for the design, introduction and implementation of non-guaranteed lifetime retirement income arrangements", in *OECD Pensions Outlook 2022*, OECD Publishing, Paris, https://doi.org/10.1787/1f1cdca9-en. [10]

OECD (2022), *Recommendation of the Council for the Good Design of Defined Contribution Pension Plans*, https://legalinstruments.oecd.org/en/instruments/OECD-LEGAL-0467. [7]

OECD (2020), "Sustainable risk sharing in retirement income arrangements", in *OECD Pensions Outlook 2020*, OECD Publishing, Paris, https://doi.org/10.1787/4c996181-en. [21]

OECD (2019), "Are funded pensions well designed to adapt to non-standard forms of work?", in *Pensions at a Glance 2019: OECD and G20 Indicators*, OECD Publishing, Paris, https://doi.org/10.1787/1231a36d-en. [2]

OECD (2019), "Non-standard forms of work and pensions", in *Pensions at a Glance 2019: OECD and G20 Indicators*, OECD Publishing, Paris, https://doi.org/10.1787/5ffa7926-en. [1]

OECD (2019), *OECD Reviews of Pension Systems: Peru*, OECD Reviews of Pension Systems, OECD Publishing, Paris, https://doi.org/10.1787/e80b4071-en. [14]

OECD (2016), "Civil service pensions: Toward a unified system with the private sector", in *OECD Pensions Outlook 2016*, OECD Publishing, Paris, https://doi.org/10.1787/pens_outlook-2016-9-en. [3]

OECD (2016), *OECD Core Principles of Private Pension Regulation*, OECD Publishing, Paris, https://doi.org/10.1787/c950bb36-en. [11]

Roser, M. (2024), *Fertility Rate*, https://ourworldindata.org/fertility-rate. [18]

## Notes

[1] Czechia, Finland, Ireland, Israel, Korea, Luxembourg, Norway, Poland.

[2] Austria, Canada, Greece, Israel, Italy, Japan, Luxembourg, New Zealand, Portugal, Spain, Türkiye.

[3] Simple average across selected countries where data is available, not weighted by assets invested.

[4] This means there are 10 individuals over age 64 for every 100 working age people between the ages of 15 and 64.

www.ingramcontent.com/pod-product-compliance
Lightning Source LLC
LaVergne TN
LVHW060456061126
851857LV00016B/1846
*9789264912311*